The Radical Practice of

Loving
Everyone

*a four-legged
approach to
enlightenment*

Michael J. Chase

W0010963

HAY HOUSE

Carlsbad, California • New York City • London • Sydney
Johannesburg • Vancouver • Hong Kong • New Delhi

First published and distributed in the United Kingdom by:
Hay House UK Ltd, Astley House, 33 Notting Hill Gate, London W11 3JQ
Tel: +44 (0)20 3675 2450; Fax: +44 (0)20 3675 2451
www.hayhouse.co.uk

Published and distributed in the United States of America by:
Hay House Inc., PO Box 5100, Carlsbad, CA 92018-5100
Tel: (1) 760 431 7695 or (800) 654 5126
Fax: (1) 760 431 6948 or (800) 650 5115
www.hayhouse.com

Published and distributed in Australia by:
Hay House Australia Ltd, 18/36 Ralph St, Alexandria NSW 2015
Tel: (61) 2 9669 4299; Fax: (61) 2 9669 4144
www.hayhouse.com.au

Published and distributed in the Republic of South Africa by:
Hay House SA (Pty) Ltd, PO Box 990, Witkoppen 2068
Tel/Fax: (27) 11 467 8904
www.hayhouse.co.za

Published and distributed in India by:
Hay House Publishers India, Muskaan Complex, Plot No.3, B-2,
Vasant Kunj, New Delhi 110 070
Tel: (91) 11 4176 1620; Fax: (91) 11 4176 1630
www.hayhouse.co.in

Distributed in Canada by:
Raincoast, 9050 Shaughnessy St, Vancouver BC V6P 6E5
Tel: (1) 604 323 7100; Fax: (1) 604 323 2600

Copyright © 2013 by Michael J. Chase

The moral rights of the author have been asserted.

Cover design: Michael J. Chase • *Interior design:* Jenny Richards

The information given in this book should not be treated as a substitute for
professional medical advice; always consult a medical practitioner. Any use
of information in this book is at the reader's discretion and risk. Neither the
author nor the publisher can be held responsible for any loss, claim or damage arising out of the use, or misuse, of the suggestions made, the failure to
take medical advice or for any material on third party websites.

A catalogue record for this book is available from the British Library.

ISBN: 978-1-78180-078-2

Printed and bound in Great Britain by TJ International, Padstow, Cornwall.

The Radical Practice of

Loving
Everyone

Also by Michael J. Chase

am I being kind

Hay House Titles of Related Interest

YOU CAN HEAL YOUR LIFE, the movie, starring Louise L. Hay
& Friends (available as a 1-DVD programme and an expanded
2-DVD set) Watch the trailer at: **www.LouiseHayMovie.com**

THE SHIFT, the movie, starring Dr Wayne W. Dyer
(available as a 1-DVD programme and an expanded 2-DVD set)
Watch the trailer at: **www.DyerMovie.com**

HEART THOUGHTS: A Daily Guide to Finding Inner Wisdom,
by Louise L. Hay

*THE MINDFUL MANIFESTO: How Doing Less and Noticing More
Can Help Us Thrive in a Stressed-out World,*
by Dr Jonty Heaversedge & Ed Halliwell

I HEART ME: The Science of Self-Love, by David R. Hamilton PhD
(available October 2013)

*SHIFT HAPPENS!: How to Live an Inspired Life . . .
Starting Right Now!,* by Robert Holden, PhD

All of the above are available at your local bookstore,
or may be ordered by visiting:

Hay House UK: **www.hayhouse.co.uk**
Hay House USA: **www.hayhouse.com**®
Hay House Australia: **www.hayhouse.com.au**
Hay House South Africa: **www.hayhouse.co.za**
Hay House India: **www.hayhouse.co.in**

For Mollie

Contents

Prologue

By day's end, her ears throbbed. The sound of clanging food dishes and slamming metal doors was agonizing. She never understood why everything had to be so loud. The keys swinging from the tall, lanky man's belt especially tortured her. His familiar shouts of, "Eat and shit! That's all you guys ever do—eat and shit!" were frequently heard up and down the hallway. That, coupled with the incessant barking of her cell mates, made her sometimes feel as if the ability to hear was a curse. She curled up into a corner and placed her oversized paws on her head, hoping to drown out the clamor.

Only one person seemed to know how to make the noises go away: the lady who flipped the three switches next to the escape door. This late-day activity caused the racket to stop, but it also made everything go dark. Instantly. At first, the silence that followed the darkness was comforting, but it also meant no food, colder floors, and mustering the patience to wait for the morning rituals: a bowl of dry kibble followed by the arrival of visitors.

Everything was different when the visitors were there. Loud voices became softer, cells were cleaner, and the man with 30 keys no longer yelled about eating and shitting. Once he even smiled. Everyone acted friendlier during these visits—the cell mates and especially the guards. These were the only times that made sense; they reminded her of why she'd been born. Some prisoners had been there too long and had forgotten . . . but not her. She knew. Although she was only eight weeks old, her little soul understood the significance of these meetings. One chance encounter could change everything. One deep connection would offer her the chance to fulfill her destiny. And one visitor's choice to set her free would end the suffering, revealing the very purpose of her life—to teach the world how to *love everyone.*

Introduction

Most spiritual seekers know that unconditional love is the foundation for achieving enlightenment. But as someone who's been on "the path" for a very long time, I'll admit that I sometimes wonder: *Is it really possible to love everyone in today's world?* Loving most, that's viable—but *everyone?* Over the years, I've read hundreds of self-empowerment books and tried a variety of methods that focused on how to accomplish this . . . but it still remained a mystery to me.

Since the answer was unclear, I decided to ask a new question. Instead of focusing on *how,* I began to ask, *Who? Who do I know that exudes the qualities of a great spiritual master—a person who lives in the present moment, is detached from the material world, embraces simplicity, has the joyful heart of a child, and loves without condition?* Being surrounded by so many deep and philosophical friends, I figured there must be someone in my life with these traits. For days I reflected on this question. I knew that there had to be someone I'd met who radiated unconditional love. Then, when I least expected it, something miraculous happened: the answer I had been searching for literally walked up to me and . . . licked my face.

Meet Mollie—an unusual and unruly standard poodle who looks more like a disheveled sheepdog than a purebred. She is 50 pounds of fluffy love. Even though she's been my constant companion over the past eight years, I didn't realize that she has been the *who* and the *how* I had been searching for all along. Looking back, I now see that her lessons have shown me that it *is possible* to live with a heart wide open—even in today's modern and sometimes unkind world. Each day I witness this phenomenon as she greets family, friends, and especially complete strangers with warmth and enthusiasm. No fear. No judgment. And no worries about what others may think of her crazy hair and zest for life—only love and affection toward all.

This book is a unique look into the soul of one four-legged guru who demonstrates the characteristics needed to *love everyone*. The following true stories share our journey together and my own attempt to emulate the very qualities that allow Mollie to live as an enlightened being.

That being said, Mollie is no angel. Unconditionally loving, yes. Well behaved . . . not always.
She is an unusual creature. Her ability to send me
from blissed to pissed (and vice versa) is an extraordinary talent. In Part I, I tell the story of how I met
Mollie and try to explain her exasperating behavior
—sometimes hysterical, often frustrating, yet in the
end enlightening. In Part II, I share our adventures
together, most of which happened during the summertime while I was writing this book. In these
chapters, I begin to recognize the spiritual lessons
she offers, as well as insights learned from the other
"gurus" we've met along the way. Part III summa-
rizes our journey together and my new approach to
life, love, and what matters most. By actually living
out Mollie's four-legged approach to enlightenment,
I can tell you that everything and everyone now
looks completely different to me—and by the end of
this book, I am certain that you'll feel this way, too.

Nineteenth-century American humorist Josh
Billings once said, "A dog is the only thing on earth
that loves you more than he loves himself." Perhaps
this is because dogs have no sense of self, therefore
making selfish behavior inconceivable. They also
seem to understand the primary reasons for why they
exist—to bring joy and love to the lives of others.

These twin purposes are also human nature. It makes no difference whether you are a person standing upright or a four-footed creature happily chasing Frisbees in the backyard. I believe that we all emanated from a source that *loves everyone*. Maybe the result of spelling *dog* backward is no coincidence after all.

PART I

In the Beginning Was the Word . . . and the Word Was *Dog*

Chapter 1

The Cookie Thief

She looked like a Tasmanian devil, spinning recklessly and carving her way through freshly fallen snow. My two friends and I, on the other hand, looked like The Three Stooges, slipping and sliding down the driveway as Mollie zigzagged between us. We circled, dove at her, and even yelled out the magic words, "Come get a cookie!" Nothing worked. As my wife, Cara, looked down from the third-floor window of our apartment, I knew I was a dead man. The mother of all Mollie incidents was unfolding, and Cara had a bird's-eye view.

I had just broken rule number one—*never let Mollie off her leash*. The truth is, I had done it countless times (not to my wife's knowledge), and, eventually,

I'd get Mollie to come back to me. Not today. I assumed the deep snow would have corralled her—or at the very least slowed her down. I was wrong. She was now sprinting like a dog that had just gulped down a double espresso.

After doing several laps around Larry, Curly, and me, Mollie became bored. She needed a bigger challenge, and hearing the UPS truck pull into the driveway across the street stopped her dead in her tracks as her head swung around. Then, as if someone had fired a starter gun at a marathon, *she was gone!* In a split second, Mollie's powerful legs were pumping, launching her body down the driveway. Her oversized ears flapped in the wind as if they were wings propelling her through the cold December air.

She charged past the UPS truck and went straight for our neighbor's backyard. Running full speed, she plowed the fresh snow with her nose. Her face, now frosted in white, had a perfect Santa beard surrounding her frozen snout. As if on a stage, she would occasionally stop long enough to make sure her audience was watching. The slightest attempt on my part to get close only sent her farther away. I swear she was laughing at me as she pranced around the yard.

Thankfully, we knew that these particular neighbors would never hear the commotion. Now in their mid-80s, the four-foot-something Greek sisters ". . .

couldn't hear a dump truck driving through a nitro-glycerin plant" (to quote one of my favorite lines from *National Lampoon's Christmas Vacation*). They are the sweetest ladies you'd ever meet but complete-ly oblivious to anything happening outside of their kitchen, especially when *The Price Is Right* is on TV.

While we continued chasing Mollie through the backyard, the UPS driver attempted to make his de-livery. It took several tries, but after pounding on the door while simultaneously ringing the doorbell, he had finally managed to get the attention of our neigh-bors. At this point, the driver balanced the sisters' ex-travagant Christmas gift—a new, 60-inch flat-screen TV—that was now wedged between his body and the porch railing. Slowly shuffling to the door, both women peered out the window. Seeing a nice-looking man dressed in brown, they unlocked the door. *Click.* Mollie's ears perked up. Her eyes widened. And I said to myself, "Oh shit . . . she's going in."

We tried to stop her, but once again Mollie dart-ed between our outstretched hands, this time racing straight for the front steps. As the UPS driver tried to maneuver the TV inside, my friends and I frantically yelled, "Close the door! Close the door!" Looking back at us with confusion, he said, "Whaaat?" We screamed again, "The door . . . close it . . . quick!" But it was too late. He had no clue that there was a 50-pound snowball coming straight at him. When Mollie dove through the gap between his legs, he finally realized what the shouting was all about. I couldn't believe my eyes as I watched her tail disappear around the corner and out of sight. Mollie was now inside the house, and there was no telling what would happen.

By the time I made it to the front door, Mollie was long gone. Red faced and out of breath, I made my way into the kitchen. One of the sisters was sitting at the table while the other leaned on the counter. A tiny, 13-inch TV to their left blared, "Come on dooowwwn! You're the next contestant on *The Price Is Right!*" They definitely needed a new TV.

I was totally embarrassed but had to ask: "Uh . . . hi there . . . did you see a dog come through here?"

The woman at the table looked up at me, smiling and with no concern whatsoever. Cookie crumbs covered her lips. Her sister turned away from the TV and said, "Oh, she's just beautiful."

I waited for more information, but that was it. So I spoke again: "Thank you. But do you happen to know which way she may have gone?"

Again, she reiterated, "What a pretty dog you have."

In my head I was screaming, *Holy crap, lady! Mollie is going to tear your freakin' house down!* But instead, I took in a deep breath and calmly said, "Okay. I think I'll just take a look around."

The house wasn't very big—just large enough for a delinquent poodle to hide in. I started calling out, "Mooollliiie, where are you? Come on, girl. Do you want a cookie?" Nothing. I looked up the stairs leading to the bedrooms. I called her name again, "Mollie, come get a cookie!" There was still no sign of her. I began to walk down a long hallway covered in '70s shag carpeting. Looking down, I found my first clue. Crumbs. There were just a few at first, but the farther I walked, the thicker the trail became. Small crumbs turned into large, gooey chunks. The evidence was everywhere. I soon discovered why Mollie hadn't responded to the treats I offered— she'd found her own.

The trail ended at a five-foot-high, plastic Christmas tree with Mollie lying underneath, head buried between the presents. Saliva-soaked wrapping paper and half-eaten cookies covered the living room floor. Despite my entrance, she continued shredding through bags of home-baked gifts. "Mollie!" I screamed. She looked back at me, smiling, with globs of biscotti stuck to her teeth. She obviously had not read the tags marked Do Not Open Until December 25th. I was horrified. She had just destroyed at least several days' worth of baking and over a dozen Christmas gifts.

While in the middle of saying "You little . . ." I quickly swallowed the last part of my sentence when the sisters walked into the room. Mollie's sugar-and-flour-laced tongue dangled from the side of her mouth. Busted. There was no denying what had happened. Looking back at the women, I grabbed Mollie by the collar, trying to find the right words to express how sorry I was. But before I could say a thing, the oldest sister joyfully exclaimed, "Oh, look how much she likes my cookies! What a *gooood* girl!"

Her sister beamed back, "Yes, she *loooves* them—give her some to take home!" They smiled and laughed while I sighed with relief, thankful that neither of them indicated that they'd be taking us to canine court.

As usual, Mollie had gotten off easy. But it would be a different story for me—my judge, jury, and executioner all rolled into one was still waiting for me across the street. And as I walked back toward my own doghouse, I fantasized about tying a red bow around Mollie's neck and asking the UPS driver, "How much would it cost to ship a poodle to the North Pole?"

Chapter 2

The Rescue Mission

The anticipation of this day was greater than any I could recall in years. It was October 9, 2004. After spending weeks researching online and begging my wife, "Can we pleeeease get a dog?" I had finally found a place that had the breed and color options we were looking for. At first, Cara was hesitant about owning a "Fifi" dog, but I assured her that not all poodles look like the ones they train for the circus—if you let their hair grow out evenly, they actually look more like a teddy bear than a show dog. We also knew that because of my allergies, a hypoallergenic pet with the least amount of dander was our sole choice.

Being an only child, my son, Alex, envisioned a puppy as a new baby brother or sister. Being an outdoorsman, I fantasized about having a new fishing buddy. And being a realist, my wife simply hoped that she wouldn't be the one doing the work. Feeding, walking, brushing, and training would soon become added tasks to our already busy life. But I promised Cara that most of the puppy chores would be mine—especially keeping the yard clear of land mines!

Finally, the day I'd been waiting for had arrived. There was an indescribable feeling of excitement in the car. After a four-hour drive into the boondocks, we were now just moments away from what was sure to be a magical land of dancing dogs. I'd pictured it all day—a wave of puppies would rush toward our car, wagging their tails, leaping and welcoming us to their country home. My mind raced with potential name choices and the thought of all the new toys we could buy. I'd also need to buy a doggy life-vest. Fishing season wouldn't end for another seven weeks, and I couldn't wait for my new friend to join me on the water.

Driving through the front gate, I was beside myself, perhaps even a little giddy. We had arrived! But, as we turned the corner and pulled up to the building . . . my heart immediately collapsed into my stomach. I was in total disbelief. Looking over at Cara, I could see that she felt the same way. Her expression appeared to say, "Turn the car around right now."

The breeder's place looked more like a prison camp from a war movie than the "Disney World for dogs" impression given on the website. Broken-down cars and dilapidated sheds were everywhere. Children with no shoes ran amok. A rusty chain-link fence surrounded dozens of barking hostages. Each one's insistent yelp seemed to cry out the same thing: "Get me the hell *outta* here!" The focal point of the compound, a large, blue-and-gray building, had the genuine look and feel you'd expect from a penal complex. It soon became obvious that this facility had all the components of a puppy mill—a breeding operation where profits take precedence over the dogs' welfare. What was supposed to be an adoption now felt more like a rescue mission.

An elfin, barefoot guard quickly brought us to the warden, who interestingly enough had the same characteristics as the prisoners. Her elongated nose and round eyes were surrounded by a 1980-something-looking perm, which hung loosely in her face. As she extended her hand to welcome us, I had mixed feelings. I desperately wanted to bring home a new puppy, but seeing these horrible conditions brought out the skeptic and judgmental tendencies in me. Over and over I thought, *I don't trust this lady who's responsible for this filthy establishment.* I especially disliked the idea of giving her our hard-earned money and wondered if this whole operation was even legal.

As unsettling as it was to see the grounds outside, the inside was much worse. As we walked through the building, we noticed that the prisoners, separated by color, were surrounded by concrete walls and thick metal bars. Each cell block held dozens of black, white, and gray pups, and even a handful with reddish coats. Big, wide eyes peered out from between the bars, gazing deep into the soul of anyone who dared to make eye contact. Immediately, I started to fantasize about doing a Rambo-like mission—sneaking in late at night, opening the gates, and setting them all free.

Earlier in the week, Cara had explained our dog preferences over the phone to the owner. She knew we wanted a standard (the largest of the breed) and, if possible, the less-common apricot color we'd seen online. Understanding our wishes, she guided us to a small room, which emitted the sounds of a canine choir. As we walked through the door, eight whirling balls of fur immediately greeted us. The sight of them would have melted the iciest of hearts and brought the toughest guy to his knees. While they danced around our feet, Cara looked at me, and we both had the exact same thought: *How will we ever choose?*

Seeing these puppies brought on a feeling of excitement . . . but also a bit of dread. The thought of leaving any of them behind in these miserable conditions was quite disheartening. We knew we could only choose one. *But how?* They were all so damn cute! My son and I quickly became fixated on one little guy who was pure energy—ears flapping, tail wagging, the whole bit. He seemed perfect. Bouncing from wall to wall, he appeared to be saying, "Look at me! Look at me! I am *soooo* much fun!" We were hooked.

Cara, however, was not as interested in our selection. She'd noticed that there was a red-haired loner sitting under a chair. What we thought was a choice between eight actually turned out to be nine. And unlike the wild guy Alex and I were playing with, this tiny pup was bashfully hiding from everyone in the room. She even looked downright depressed. The only things more pitiful than her droopy ears were her sad brown eyes.

Bending down with apprehension, my wife gently picked up number nine and placed it on her lap.

While caressing the puppy's head, Cara looked at the warden and asked, "Is there anything wrong with this one? She seems sad." In a nonchalant tone, the woman slowly replied, "Oh, her . . . she's just a little dim. Her lightbulb will come on in a week or so." Having heard that, Cara's motherly instincts kicked in. She wouldn't even look at the others. She was determined to save number nine, and a duel was about to begin.

It was my high-energy pup versus her slowpoke—mine was regular and hers was decaf. Their personalities were like night and day. Alex and I argued that we wanted a playful puppy, not a dud, but Cara was only interested in a sweet little girl to sit on her lap and spoil. For several minutes we argued our cases back and forth. It was a dead heat. But this seemingly impossible decision was about to be made for us. Not by a coin toss or the warden's input, but rather, by my very own contender. The dog Alex and I had chosen suddenly stopped running so he could *go*. And go. And go. We all stood there in shock. There was obviously something wrong with him. My wife saw this incident (or accident) as a sign and took it as an opportunity to close the deal. As the prison guards mopped up the runny evidence, Cara gently placed her tiny friend into my arms. The warm sensation of puppy breath on my skin had me against the ropes, but I wasn't giving in. *Male dogs are more playful,* I erroneously thought. Besides, I was sure that my guy only needed a little doggie Pepto-Bismol. I continued to stand my ground even when Cara's choice pressed her nose up to my chin. I was thoroughly convinced that there was no way I could lose this battle . . . until I made the ultimate rookie mistake—I looked down into her soft brown eyes. That was all it took. My heart instantly melted. Seconds later, my nose was buried in her fur as I was kissing the top of her head, talking to her the way a parent gushes over a new baby. It was official: I was now head over heels in love with number nine, and she was going home with us. To this day, I'm still not sure who picked whom. . . .

Chapter 3

One Sick Puppy

After much deliberation, we decided to call her Mollie. And as proud parents, we did what all others do—we put her on display for everyone to see. During the first few days, we e-mailed photos to family and friends, paraded her throughout the neighborhood, and pretty much turned our life into one big show-and-tell. Each day became a new opportunity for us to brag that *we* had the world's cutest puppy.

There was no denying that Mollie was adorable. She turned heads everywhere she went. But after the first week had gone by, something didn't seem right. Her "lightbulb," as the breeder had put it, was yet to come on. We thought she'd be a bit more energetic at this point, but that wasn't the case. Rather than play with the 50 toys (I'm only slightly exaggerating) we'd purchased for her, Mollie would sit quietly by herself under the kitchen table leaning on her "kickstand," which is what we nicknamed her back right leg, because it often served as the primary support for her body as she sat, tilting to one side. It was a sad sight.

Shortly after we brought Mollie home, she was scheduled to get her first set of shots. In the waiting area of the vet's office, she sat quietly on Cara's lap. When it was her turn, Cara placed Mollie on the examination table. Within minutes of meeting Mollie, the doctor said, "Something isn't right here. A puppy shouldn't be this lethargic." The concern in his voice immediately made us feel anxious. The doctor decided that Mollie was too weak to receive her shots and that we should wait a few days to see if she might be coming down with something. We were devastated. Seeing her sad little face broke our hearts. Our new dog wasn't "dim"; she was sick.

At the same time, I also had a few health issues of my own to deal with. Ever since returning from puppy prison, my allergies had gone ballistic on me. The sneezing was uncontrollable, and my bloodshot eyes made me look as if I had a serious drug problem—

which, in reality, I did! My problem, however, was that I couldn't find a drug that worked! Each day, I tried new antihistamines and sucked on my steroid inhaler. My sinuses were a complete mess, but it was my asthma that had everyone concerned.

A few years before, I'd had a near-death experience due to a severe asthma attack. As a result, I'd been forced to take my breathing problems much more seriously. After visiting my doctor for my current condition, she offered me a cure . . . but I declined. She said that only one thing would make all of my miseries go away: *get rid of Mollie.* Upon hearing my doctor's recommendation, Cara kindly told me, "You'll live in the basement before that happens." I don't think she was joking.

The next week was filled with more of the same—nothing helped my allergies, and Mollie was still quite frail. It was frustrating, but all we could do at this point was take the situation one day at a time. Despite continued health problems, I was excited to have my favorite fall pastime to look forward to: watching my beloved Boston Red Sox in the playoffs. Like most New Englanders, I'd spent much of my life as a devoted, glutton-for-punishment, wait-until-next-year fan. To follow the Red Sox is to embrace the teachings of the Buddha and the first of the

Four Noble Truths: that life is inherently full of suffering. Each October as the playoffs rolled around, I hoped and I prayed; but in the end, the Sox always let me down. The 86-year-old curse that had denied them a World Series title was still intact, and the fall of 2004 seemed to be no different. As usual, they were blowing it.

On October 16th, the Buddha's wisdom rang especially true, as things for Mollie and the entire Red Sox Nation went from bad to worse. During game three of the American League Championship (a 19-8 thrashing of the Sox by the New York Yankees), Cara noticed that something was wrong with Mollie—very wrong. Her tiny body was shaking as she whimpered pitiful noises of distress. She'd been quiet for days, but this episode was unlike anything we'd seen. After contacting a late-night emergency clinic, we were soon in the car, exceeding the speed limit to cut time from our drive. Mollie's motionless body now lay curled up on Cara's lap as we prayed the whole way there. It was obvious to us that her health, like that of her littermates, had been severely compromised by starting her life in such an unsanitary environment.

After finally arriving and filling out the required paperwork, the three of us went through the agonizing process of waiting. It made no difference wheth-er you were a bulldog filled with porcupine quills or a little poodle puppy with the shakes; you had to wait. Each passing moment felt like an hour. To make matters worse, the TV was on, rubbing the Red Sox's embarrassing loss in our face. The next night would have them facing an elimination game—no team had ever come back to win a playoff series after being down three games to one. "You guys suck," I muttered under my breath. The lowly Red Sox were now the least important thing in my life, so I decid-ed to stop wasting my prayers on them and instead turn my attention to Mollie. She needed it more. Only this time I was going to ask for a full-blown miracle. . . .

After the vet gave Mollie a potentially lifesaving shot, her condition began to improve the very next day. She was now on medication and starting to be-come more active, and that's not all. As the week went on, it seemed that my prayer for a miracle had been met with a gigantic, "Yes!" Apparently, God was no longer a New York Yankees fan—the "evil empire" was now in the midst of a momentous col-lapse. Night after night, with Mollie close by my side, we witnessed one magical moment after an-other as the Boston Red Sox completed the greatest comeback in baseball history. It was unbelievable—they were going to the World Series! Sure, there was still the possibility that they could choke, causing me to dig out my "wait until next year" T-shirt, but at that moment I didn't care. Life was good. In addition to Boston's trip to the Fall Classic, Mollie was acting more like a healthy, happy dog, and my allergy symptoms had all but disappeared. I asked for one miracle and had been given three.

After nearly a month of doctor visits, tests, emergency-room visits, and loads of stress (related to health and baseball), everything had come full circle. On Wednesday, October 27, 2004, Mollie and I shared an unprecedented moment in history—we watched the Red Sox win the 100th World Series. With Mollie resting on my lap, I choked back tears while my favorite players danced on the stadium field. To some, it may seem silly for a grown man to cry over baseball, but my new four-legged best friend didn't seem to mind. Bending forward, I kissed the top of her head and could only utter the words, "We did it, girl. We really did it."

Chapter 4

How Bad Can She Be?

What we thought was going to be a Lassie-like experience of raising a dog turned into one insane event after another. The words, "Kennel! Go to your kennel right now!" echoed throughout the house on a daily basis. Following each incident, Mollie knew just by the look in my eyes that it was best to hightail it to solitary confinement. We'd hoped that over time her antics would subside. No such luck. Each week there seemed to be a new story to tell—like the day she ran away and was lost for an hour, or the time she was hit by a car (without any major injuries, thank God!). Days like these had us on a first-name basis with the staff at every emergency clinic in southern Maine. Often, Mollie's tricks involved stealing a dish towel from the kitchen sink or running through the halls with our laundry, dirty or clean, but some days were worse. Much worse.

One particular evening, I was sitting on the couch watching TV while Cara sat beside me working on a quilt. (I'm always amazed by how she can take a pile of material, cut it up, and sew it into something that looks as if it belongs in a museum.) Mollie, who's curious about *anything* we're doing, had been staring at Cara longingly in hopes that whatever she was making would turn into a tug toy. Perhaps more than being curious, she was just plain bored; since it had rained all week, she'd been trapped indoors other than quick runs out for bathroom breaks. Without her daily exercise, Mollie turned into a juvenile delinquent.

As I channel surfed, Cara continued the tedious process of hand sewing the edges of her latest art piece. Finally stopping to give her fingers a quick break, she reached over to drop her sewing needle into the basket on the end table. At this exact moment, Mollie leaped up, stuck her head in the basket, and ran out of the room. She skidded down the hallway and ran headfirst into her kennel. We watched in disbelief as the scene unfolded in the blink of an eye. Then Cara screamed frantically as she searched the basket, hoping that what she was thinking had not actually happened. "Oh my God! I think she swallowed my needle! It's not here! I can't find it!"

Within the first two years since Mollie had joined our family, she'd devoured numerous rocks, fully wrapped snack bars, CDs, plum pits, a loaf of bread defrosting on the counter, and even an entire gourmet cheese ball, just to name a few. Consuming everything in sight was par for the course, but nothing like this had ever happened before, and this latest episode had us scared to death.

Cara scoured the floor, hoping Mollie had dropped the needle during her getaway. I went straight for the kennel. The scene of me crawling inside this tiny box was all too familiar. But this was unlike the usual task of pulling a sock or my favorite hat from her jaws. The stakes were much higher, and time was of the essence. I also knew that aggressive body language was not a good idea. One wrong move, and this could end very badly. For me to be able to open Mollie's mouth, I would first need to coax her into turning her body around. Whenever she ran into her two-by-three-foot house, she always put her head in the corner like a punished child. This was also her way of hiding the saliva-covered evidence in the back of the kennel where I couldn't reach it.

As I pulled her long body out, I gently grabbed her snout. Using my hands like the Jaws of Life, I began the always-difficult task of trying to pry open her mouth, which is like a steel trap. Finally, I got it open and began to fish around, searching for the needle. Nothing. I opened her mouth wider to look down her throat. Still nothing. Not even a piece of thread. I started to think to myself, *She must have dropped it. It must be on the floor, somewhere between here and the living room.* Besides, the whole notion of her actually swallowing a sewing needle now seemed crazy, even impossible to some extent.

Cara eventually made her way down the hall to where I was holding Mollie hostage. Almost hysterical, she cried out, "Did you find it?! Was it in her mouth?"

"No, I can't find it anywhere," I replied.

After thoroughly checking Mollie again, we continued looking on the floor, in the kennel, and every other place a stray needle could have fallen. Cara even did her chant to the patron saint of lost things, St. Anthony. This was customary whenever an item in our home was missing in action, and it involved a heartfelt plea of, "Dear St. Anthony, please look around. There's something lost that must be found."

Thirty minutes later, there was still no needle or any real indication that Mollie had actually swallowed it. She seemed to be acting normally, yet we weren't totally convinced that this razor-sharp sewing tool hadn't found its way down Mollie's throat. So rather than take any chances, we called the emergency clinic.

Since it was late in the evening, the vet had told us that it was best to keep Mollie home. In the morning, we could make arrangements for x-rays and, if necessary . . . surgery. For now, we just needed to keep her calm and all try and get a good night of sleep. We guided Mollie to her kennel, which was in the bedroom next to ours. Then we both gave her a hug and said a little prayer. Cara was still noticeably anxious, and I was a bit nervous, too, but mostly convinced the rogue needle would be found when we had better light the next morning. *Surely it had rolled under the refrigerator or was lodged in a darkened corner of the hallway,* I optimistically thought.

Around 2 A.M., the familiar sound of hacking and retching emanated from the next room. Cara immediately sprang from the bed and headed for Mollie. I followed, stumbling through the darkness as I heard the unpleasant sound of regurgitation. As we unlocked the kennel door, we were met by our puppy, who was engaged in a full-body heave. Nothing had come up yet, but it was certainly on its way. Every time Mollie gets sick, it's like watching a space shuttle launch, and at that moment we were in the final seconds of the countdown. *Seven, six . . .* her muscles tensed up . . . *five, four . . .* I rubbed her belly, trying to comfort her . . . *three, two . . .* she pointed her head down . . . *one. Whooooosh . . . Houston, we have a problem.* And there it was. Using my fingers to dig through the goopy slime, I felt the sharpened point of the needle. Still looped through its eye was the green thread Cara had been using. Looking at the two-inch piece of metal, I was in pure awe. How it slid down and then made its way back up my dog's throat without lodging itself was a miracle—an absolute *miracle.*

Over time, we started to realize that Mollie's behavior was just a part of who she was—a totally crazy dog. This was her personality, and there was nothing we could do to change it. We'd tried obedience class, but that didn't work. She ended up being the star (not in a good way) and was voted class clown. The teacher couldn't help but laugh at her.

It was always something with Mollie, such as the time we went on a family camping trip in northern Maine. Mollie loves the water, which is why she has to be leashed when we go to the lake, to avoid upsetting the locals. Seeing her dive off the dock isn't a big deal to me, but chasing after the neighbors' boats, well, that's another story.

On this particular day, the ten-foot rope I had tied to a tree was long enough to cure Mollie's separation anxiety, but just short enough to keep her out of trouble. Or so I thought. Mollie is the ultimate opportunist. Her heightened sense of awareness and radarlike nose always have her searching for a snack, and the next one was just a few feet away.

Walking down the sloped gravel driveway, my friend's three-year-old daughter, Kayleigh, was slowly making her way toward the water. This little girl looks like a doll—big blue eyes, long curly hair, and always giggling. Wearing her *Dora the Explorer* bathing suit, she wobbled down the hill with one hand holding a bucket for catching tadpoles while the other hand loosely gripped a pink glazed donut. It was the prize of the box, and she had yet to take a bite.

Mollie loves kids. She can feel their energy and relates to their playful spirit. Knowing this, I never worry about her being around children. Sure, she can be mischievous, but she would never hurt anyone. Perhaps I should rephrase that last statement: Mollie would never *physically* hurt someone—but as far as never hurt their feelings, that's something I can't guarantee.

Upon seeing Kayleigh, Mollie perked up. They had just met the day before but were already best friends. As the toddler approached, Mollie went from sitting upright to standing on all fours with her tail wagging. It was as if she was smiling, with the reflection of pink sugar now gleaming in her eyes. Still, I wasn't worried. The rope was ten feet long, and Kayleigh was now . . . *nine feet and eleven inches away.*

Standing on her hind legs, Mollie suspended her body, stretching out the last inch needed to obtain the most sought-after item of this little girl's day. And in one giant bite, the *last pink glazed donut on Earth* had disappeared. Well, I can only assume that it was the last one on Earth due to Kayleigh's reaction. Her screams of *"Moooollllliiiieeee tooook mmmmyyyy doooonuttttt!"* reverberated like the painful echo of a tripped car alarm. How such a tiny body could emit that much noise is actually an extraordinary phenomenon. With no remorse, Mollie sat there pink lipped and grinning, her expression appearing to say, *Hey, thanks for sharing your breakfast with me!* The entire lake now knew about our catastrophic event.

I guess I should have been more sensitive regarding Kayleigh's dilemma, perhaps even offered to drive back to the bakery to replace the holy grail of pastries. But the truth is, I only had one regret: *Ten million hits on YouTube . . . if I'd only had a camera . . . ten million hits.*

Chapter 5

The Road Less Traveled

Now at the ripe old age of eight, Mollie pretty much lives to the beat of her own drum. Cara and I tried for years to teach (or bribe) her to act like a "real dog," but we finally had to let go of that fantasy. It's just not going to happen, mostly because Mollie refuses to accept the fact that having four legs and a tail means that she isn't a human. Just one look into her eyes, and you'd swear you're looking at a person—perhaps a reincarnated comedian or actress that passed away many lifetimes ago. She definitely has a flair for the dramatic and loves to be in the spotlight.

Some might say that Mollie is spoiled. Unlike the early years, she no longer sleeps in her kennel.

Seeing her sad face behind bars at night finally broke us. Now, depending on the temperature and time of year, she bounces between our bed, the floor, and sometimes the living-room couch. Throughout the winter months, she's typically on the bed, making herself quite comfortable at our expense. Mollie's habit of lying across (or on top of) Cara and me makes it rather difficult to sleep. Sometimes, she will lie between us, stretch her body parallel with ours, and place her head on my pillow. We look like three sardines lined up in a row. And if Cara or I should happen to get out of bed during the night to use the bathroom, Mollie seizes the opportunity to steal our spot. This is simply another way of her letting us know that she is *not* a dog.

During the warmer months Mollie will usually give us a break by taking the floor. Still, being off the bed doesn't mean that we've regained any power. She makes the rules. Usually somewhere just before 5 A.M., Mollie will rise up from the floor, stretch, stare at us for about ten seconds . . . and begin to cluck. Yes, cluck—like a chicken. She knows better than to do her customary, vivacious bark at such an early hour, so instead she begins a series of *bock, bock, bock* noises, informing us that it's time to get up. But on some mornings, when you just want to stay in bed, this can be maddening! "Mollie, that's enough," I'll often snap at her . . . to which she then looks back at me, gets into her diva stance, and replies, "Bock, bock, bock!" There's no reasoning with her. When Mollie says it's time to get up, it's time to get up.

Our morning routine is pretty much the same each day. I make my way to the kitchen to put on some coffee. Once the "smell" of caffeine is in the air, I then click on the local news, check the weather, and take my clucking dog outside to pee. When her business is done, it's back inside to prepare for the day's most ludicrous and unpredictable task— feeding Mollie.

For several years now, Mollie has made breakfast an absurd occasion. Despite the fact that she will eat anything remotely edible off the floor, tables, and streets, she often rejects the high-quality dog food we offer her. More specifically, she declines it as is. Unless we sprinkle in a little Parmesan cheese or crush a peanut-butter cookie on top of her chow, she won't give it a second look. Then there are days when the extra toppings make no difference whatsoever. She simply turns her nose up as if to say, "Please send this back and tell the chef I am never dining here again." There are also times when my wife rolls kibble to Mollie one piece at a time while she sits six feet away. Oh, but it gets better. Perhaps the most ridiculous thing I've ever witnessed was seeing my wife on the floor with Mollie in front of her (get ready for this one) being *spoon-fed one scoop at a time!* Un-freaking-believable.

While the battle over breakfast is going on, I'm often in a downward-dog pose, getting in my 40 minutes of yoga. This daily practice has been completely life changing for me. It's also the perfect way to prepare for the morning's next big adventure—walking Mollie. Compared to incessant clucking, and even spoon-feeding, walking her is an experience unlike any other. It's crazy, erratic, hysterical, frustrating . . . and my favorite part of the day.

Morning strolls are not as simple as leashing up the dog and running out the door. It's a process. My walking partner is always eager to go, but upon seeing the dreaded Easy Walk Harness, she does a complete 360-degree turn, bobbing and weaving away from me like a lightweight boxer being chased in the ring. But this is one argument that she *will not* win. The standard collar-and-leash approach has never worked with her. Ever. It gave her too much freedom to pull me, dart into traffic, jump up and hug complete strangers, and eat everything in her path.

We always try to leave the house by 6:30 A.M. to beat the school traffic. For me, walking is about feeling relaxed and clearing my head for the new day. I love the peace and quiet that the morning offers. Therefore, the sound of a teenager's pimped-out Mazda racing toward the high school is the last thing I want to hear at sunrise. A walk for Mollie is more about meeting new people or occasionally finding a chunk of bagel on the ground. She won't eat her fancy dog food, but a dried-up piece of bread covered in ants—*yuummmy!*

For some time now, Mollie and I have taken a very specific 45-minute route—the most drama-free one. After moving into a new neighborhood, we quickly learned which streets were best for avoiding excess traffic and, especially, less-than-kind dogs. We've had our fair share of encounters with pooches that do not practice unconditional love.

One particular morning, ten minutes into our walk Mollie put on the brakes for her first "morning doo." Invariably, she always likes to choose a spot near a traffic light or wherever as many people as possible can watch me bend over and scoop up last night's dinner. Thankfully, on this day she decided to go near an intersection where a trash receptacle was just a few feet away. I had strategically mapped out our walk to ensure I would never have to carry a smelly bag for long. Mollie, now in full squat mode, did her thing while a few onlookers drove by. She was not the least bit embarrassed. I, of course, awkwardly looked away. Jerry Seinfeld's brilliant observation says it all: "[D]ogs are the leaders. If you see two life forms, one of them making a poop, and the other one's carrying it for him, who would you assume is in charge?" Poop or no poop, if Jerry ever meets Mollie, he'll have no doubt that she's in charge.

With the least pleasant part of our morning now over, we were on the road again, heading through the neighborhoods we frequent each day. Before we left, I'd checked the weather to make sure the forecasted rain would hold off for a while. The entire time Mollie and I were out, there was dampness in the air but no rain had fallen. With only 20 minutes left in our walk, it appeared that we'd be safe. Then, just as we were about to turn a corner—the same corner, mind you, that we've taken every day for months—something happened. Actually, two things happened. First, it started to sprinkle. It wasn't enough to make me want to race home, but it was obvious that rain was on its way. Second, Mollie stopped. And I mean stopped cold. It wasn't an "it's time to get another bag ready" kind of way, but rather, "I think I'll play the role of the world's most stubborn mule." It was absurd. She dropped her butt to the ground, dug her front paws into the pavement, and simply would not budge.

So I pulled. And then I pulled some more. Her body seemed as if it were twice its weight. It was like trying to boat a marlin. She absolutely refused to move. "What's wrong with you?" I asked. Bending down, I checked her over but nothing seemed out of the ordinary. Her paws looked fine, and I could see no reason why she'd act this way. Her eyes, however, which are normally filled with wonder and pure joy, now looked intense.

Standing up, I said, "All right, Mollie. That's enough. Let's go." I yanked on her leash, but once again she dug in, only this time even deeper. In the meantime, the rain had begun to fall harder. People were beginning to stare, and I could feel my patience waning. Finally, I knelt down, got nose to nose with her, and firmly bellowed, "Come on, Mollie, let's go!" Now soaking wet and getting angrier by the second, I stood up and pulled one last time. Her eyes squinted back at me like Clint Eastwood when he was getting ready to draw his pistol in a gunfight. And as she tugged back with all her might, I blurted out something not very kind, even if it was under my breath.

As the rain picked up in intensity, Mollie's normally fluffy hair began to look and feel like a saturated rag doll. Running my hand across her head, I relented, "Okay, Mol. Tell me . . . what do *you* want to do?" While talking to her, I gently tried to persuade her my way. She resisted. I then decided to try a little bribery. After using my sleeve to wipe the rain from my face, I reached into my pocket, grabbed a treat, held out my hand, and said, "Do you want a cookie?" to which she immediately said yes by making it disappear. Still, that did nothing to move her forward. It seemed that I now had only two options left. And since I had no desire to carry a large, soaking wet poodle in my arms across town, I took the second choice. I leaned in close and asked, "Hey, girl, do you want to go a different way?" Taking a deep breath, I lightly pulled her leash in the opposite direction.

Bingo! Mollie was now wide-eyed and trotting down the sidewalk like the world's happiest dog. I had no clue what the whole fiasco had been about 30 yards back, but at that moment I didn't care. At least we were finally on the move again. And since the rain was coming down at a good clip, I decided it was best to cut our walk short and head back. But as I turned onto a street that would get us home in the least amount of time . . . she did it again. "Oh, come on, Mollie!" She had stopped, sat down, and glared back at me when I tried to move forward.

"Fine!" I exclaimed. "Which way are we going now?" Something told me to turn toward the direction her nose was pointing in. As soon as I did, she instantly sprang up and led the way.

This went on for several blocks—I'd turn south to move us closer to home, while she would go north, east, or west. Although we were both dripping wet, I was no longer mad. I couldn't help but laugh each time she took us off the beaten path. As Mollie pulled me up and down streets I'd never seen before, something profound came to mind. Although we weren't far from our normal route, it felt like a whole different world. What I'd originally perceived as stubbornness was actually her way of breaking us free from the same old habit. The streets we'd been taking before were fine, but clearly we were missing out on so much more. In the last 15 minutes, not only had we seen new homes, beautiful gardens, and a large oak tree that we used as shelter, but we'd also made several new friends along the way.

Why Mollie started this new behavior, I'll never know. But ever since that soggy day, she now surprises me during almost every walk. Sometimes it's a different street, other times it's simply crossing the road sooner than I'd planned. But rather than being frustrated, I now see this as the perfect metaphor for my life. Perhaps this is my crazy dog's way of telling me that it's time to step out of my comfort zone. Maybe older dogs really can learn new tricks.

Chapter 6

Wake-Up Call

Despite Mollie's ability to drive me mad at times, it's impossible to remain angry with her. Yes, she can be a menace, but she is also the most loving, compassionate, sweet, and gentle creature I've ever known. Unlike my attitude toward some people's behavior, forgiving Mollie is effortless. Perhaps this is because she does the same for me. If I'm too tired to take her for a walk or toss her favorite soccer ball, she never holds a grudge. Or when I yell at her, lock her in the kennel, or even steal her freedom by tying her to a leash, she always looks at me with total devotion. I've truly come to love and appreciate her not only as a pet, but as my closest friend.

The positive effect she's had on my emotional state is extraordinary. I can't begin to count the number of times she's been able to snap me out of a bad mood or give my attitude a much-needed adjustment. Sometimes it's the way she jumps up and hugs me when she greets me at the door. Other times it can be the simple act of bringing me her favorite toy, dropping it in front of me, and barking once as if to say, "Here, play with this!" But it works—every single time. Even when she steals my sandwich (note to self: stop leaving food on tables lower than four feet high), I'm angry at first, but then can't help but laugh when I see her fuzzy face covered in honey mustard as she attempts to devour a foot-long sub in one bite.

There is an unspoken (obviously) understanding between us. I've learned to accept Mollie's wild behavior, and she continues to love me in spite of my own faults, including the uncertainty that comes from being a dreamer. Such was the case in October 2007 when vast changes were taking place in our life.

As I wrote about in my first book, *am I being kind,* after 16 years as professional photographers, Cara and I had decided to close our successful studio to start a new venture called The Kindness Center. What began as a simple idea for creating events to perform random acts of kindness quickly turned into a career in writing and speaking. Soon, I was sharing the message and benefits of living a kinder life at schools, businesses, and organizations. I especially wanted to work with students. My goal was to alleviate the problems of bullying, substance abuse, and suicide. Helping teenagers make positive choices would become one of the most rewarding things I'd ever do. I realized that this was also a part of my karmic journey. Let's just say that I wasn't always the kindest kid in school.

Cara was behind me 100 percent. Others, however, were a bit concerned about how we'd make a living. What many people didn't know was that the message of kindness was very important to me. Actually, it was extremely personal. Unkindness on my father's side of the family was like a disease—a generational nightmare filled with alcohol abuse and extreme acts of violence. My great-grandfather infected my grandfather, who passed it on to my dad, and it eventually made its way to me. This trickle-down effect sent me spiraling into a whirlpool of despair throughout my childhood and well into my adult years. But it wasn't until my father's suicide (the end result of my grandfather's vicious behavior) that I woke up and began to search for an alternative path in life. I vowed to be the one to finally break the cycle, ensuring that my son would never become a part of this ugly family history.

Just three years into the new business, Cara and I were able to accomplish what many critics had deemed impossible. The response to my work was so positive that I was now beginning to travel, sharing the message of kindness in front of hundreds of people on a regular basis. Thanks to the media, my new nickname, "The Kindness Guy," started to catch on. People even recognized me out in public and would occasionally yell, "Hey, Kindness Guy!"

Unfortunately, at the same time, our financial situation had hit rock bottom. My new career was progressing, but my income was not enough to pay our bills. Keeping our heads above water was a constant struggle. "Do you take Visa?" often became our mantra as credit cards were a necessary evil for covering our living expenses. It wasn't long before we had exhausted our credit lines, used up all our savings, lost our health insurance, and liquidated our material possessions. Sadly, all we could do was pray for better days as we watched the bank foreclose on our home.

Perhaps the most telling stories from these times were the days when Cara and I had no money for food. I recall one evening digging through the drawer in search of spare change to buy a box of pasta.

Angry with God, the whole world, and especially myself, I looked at my wife and said, "I can't do this anymore. I'm done. I need a real job."

Just saying the words actually made my heart ache, but despite our situation and the stress it was creating, Cara looked at me with tears in her eyes and said, "You can't give up. We will get through this. The world needs what you're doing now more than ever. Don't worry, everything will be fine." Yes, my wife is truly amazing.

During the hard times, I have to admit that I often struggle emotionally. Financial uncertainty can wear me down, even stop me from doing the very thing that alleviates the problem—working. The next two years were not exactly easy, but thanks to the love and support of family, friends, and even complete strangers, Cara and I were able to keep our dream alive. We were also grateful that our son, Alex, was away at college during the toughest times and didn't have to see the sacrifices we made, especially when our fridge was empty.

Having *am I being kind* published was definitely a boost to my spirit. Despite that, though, by the time the following winter arrived, the recurring financial struggles were getting the best of me again. As a result, I began to feel depressed and even distanced myself from my loved ones.

Normally, I was a caring and optimistic person. But I was struggling profoundly—feeling agitated with others, the injustices of the world, and especially myself. Emotionally, it had been one of those years. Still, I knew any seeds of negativity inside of me were there by choice. I was responsible. Granted, these seeds were tiny compared to the ones that were buried inside my former self, but they were still there nonetheless.

The words of Buddhist monk and poet Thich Nhat Hanh gave me hope:

> Though we all have the seeds of fear and anger within us, we must learn not to water those seeds and instead nourish our positive qualities— compassion, understanding, and loving kindness.

I was ready to plant new seeds.

Ironically, while feeling this way, I was attempting to write a book about unconditional love—a subject that I hadn't yet mastered. This new book (what you're holding in your hands) was inspired by the final chapter in *am I being kind,* where I shared a story about my other grandfather (my mother's dad), Moppy, who was an amazing man with tremendous wit and his own unique brand of wisdom. Moppy and I were best buddies. Whether we were discussing football or randomly dueling against each other with bad knock-knock jokes, he always knew how to make me smile. Sadly, in 2007, the very week I started The Kindness Center, Moppy died of cancer. I was devastated. But fortunately, just before he passed away, I had taken the time to have a heart-to-heart conversation with him, asking his thoughts on success and living a good life. His career and material life were impressive, but I was mostly curious about his ability to attract so many friends (real friends, not Facebook friends). He had a reputation for getting along with everybody, and I wanted to know his secret.

After many hours of drinking coffee and reflecting on the ups and downs of his 80 years, I finally asked him the big question: "Gramp, why do you think you have so many friends?"

At first he just shrugged it off with a shy "Oh, I don't know," but I was relentless. I kept repeating the question until he finally broke. After thinking for a few seconds, he paused, looked down into his coffee cup, and said, "I don't know, Mike . . . I guess I just love everyone." At first his answer seemed too basic. But he stuck to it. It was his only answer—two simple, seemingly impossible words: *love everyone*.

Did this mean he was enlightened? Will this Moppy-ism ignite the next big spiritual revolution? Only if it includes smoking a pack of cigarettes a day and eating large quantities of cookies!

My grandfather was a beautiful man, but he wasn't perfect. He would have been the first one to tell you that. Even my mom, who looked at him with such reverence, admits that there were definitely a few people who drove him crazy. But looking back, I can now understand what he was saying to me. His philosophy was built on the idea of *accepting everyone*. This was his spiritual practice. He always accepted people for who they were, rather than who he thought they should be. Moppy couldn't have cared less about what people looked like; what kind of car they drove; or if they were black or white, rich or poor, Christian or Muslim, straight or gay, or Democrat or Republican (although their political views could certainly lead to a friendly debate). In his own way, he really did love everyone.

The process of writing my new book wasn't going well. For weeks I sat at my computer, waiting for the first words to come to me, but my heart wasn't into it. I stared at the cover and title that I'd created, hoping it would generate inspiration. The photo on the front was of a rolling field of tall, swaying grass sprinkled with dandelions and surrounded by trees. Cara, who's always honest with me, made it clear that she didn't care for this image. Deep down, neither did I.

Two months went by, and I had yet to write a sentence. Only two brilliant words flowed from my keyboard onto the screen: *Chapter One*. But that was it. No chapter titles, no subjects, and at this point . . . no longer a desire to write. I was done. That night I decided it was time to step away; it was just too frustrating. Here I was considered an "expert" on love and kindness, teaching it to thousands of people, yet I had nothing to say. Then I began to beat myself up, thinking that my last book was a fluke and I'd only be remembered as a one-hit wonder. I now understood what it felt like to be rap artist Vanilla Ice.

Heading to bed that night, I was disappointed but also somewhat relieved. I knew that I was burning out and needed a break. It's not always easy to accept, but sometimes surrendering is a good thing. Whether it's writer's block or the need to be right, the art of letting go is necessary for anyone who's striving for inner peace. As I drifted off to sleep, listening to one of my favorite Ram Dass lectures on my iPod, I actually felt a serenity that I hadn't experienced in a long time. I also felt that for the first time in weeks I was going to get a good night's sleep. Until . . .

. . . a French kiss that I will not soon forget woke me in the middle of the night. I mean, it was warm, wet, and the worst breath I've ever smelled. It was as if someone had hit me in the face with a sweaty sock. Instantly, I jumped up, startled from this intimate and rather unexpected moment. Cara was still on her side of the bed sleeping, so I knew it had to be the other woman in my life. Wiping the drool from my face, I screamed, "Mollie, what the hell!" I then looked at the clock, which said 2:11 A.M.

Cara rolled over and groggily asked, "What's the matter?"

Rubbing my eyes, I replied, "Nothing. Mollie just woke me up, that's all." Mollie was resting her chin on the edge of the mattress, staring at me with a big goofy smile. This was out of character for her at that hour. Occasionally, she'd wake us with a muffled bark if an unfamiliar noise came from the street, but a late-night tongue-lashing was not her style. She looked like she wanted something, but it wasn't the usual "give me a cookie" dance or an indication that she had to pee. She just stared, smiled, and wagged her tail.

Lying back down, I started to tousle the hair on top of her shaggy head, relaxing into a slumber . . . until it hit me. *Oh my God!* I thought. *That's it!* Springing from the bed, I wrapped my arms around Mollie's neck, kissed her nose, and began scrambling for a piece of paper and a pen. Curious about my burst of energy, Mollie pranced behind me as I practically ran out of the bedroom.

One inspiring thought after another flowed through my mind onto the paper in front of me. I would not be going back to sleep anytime soon. It was official—my writer's block was over. I now realized whom *The Radical Practice of Loving Everyone* was going to be about: the only one I knew who actually encompassed the qualities necessary to practice unconditional love. She was unselfish, forgiving, nonjudgmental, ego free, and always living in the present moment. These are the traits of enlightened beings! My head understood that Mollie was a dog; my heart, however, now saw her in a completely different way: as the ultimate expression of everything I wanted to be.

PART II

When the Student
Is Ready, the Teacher
Will Appear

Chapter 7

A Deeper Understanding

For a while now, I've been meeting with my friend John to learn about Tibetan Buddhism. As a practicing Buddhist, he has studied under many remarkable teachers. And it shows. John's peaceful energy, combined with a smile that could dissolve the murkiest of moods, has had me curious to know more about his journey toward enlightenment.

One particular day when John and I met for coffee, he shared one profound teaching after another, each lesson building on the next and awakening something deep in my heart. He has an amazing way of making the complex seem straightforward and accessible. But as John revealed his wisdom that morning, my mind was racing. The ideas he shared with me were so stimulating that all I cared about was getting started—I wanted the step-by-step guide for how to achieve enlightenment in one day. But each time I hinted at this desire, he invariably brought everything back to one word: *understanding.*

Over and over John would say, "It all begins with understanding . . . understanding leads to wisdom." With each teaching, he would look back at me and inquire, "Does this make sense? Do you understand?" Everything he said made total sense, which was why I was so eager for the next step! My mind screamed, *I get it, so just tell me how to be enlightened already!* But whenever I asked for the *how,* it was always met with the same response: "Remember, we're just trying to understand." It all felt like a Zen riddle or some kind of philosophical brainteaser. It also seemed that the only thing I didn't understand was *understanding.*

Before we parted, I decided to tell John about the new book I was writing, my recent revelation, and how Mollie was the inspiration behind it all. After sharing the premise, I then explained my predicament regarding Mollie's split personality—you know, how she displays many spiritual traits, but at times also drives me crazy. Smiling, John responded with delight, "That's so perfect! It makes total sense."

I waited for a punch line, but there was none. I stared back at him and thought, *Huh?*

Still grinning, he then went on to say, "Mollie is like a Tibetan lama, or guru. Once a student has begun to make a transition toward enlightenment, the guru does everything he can to drive the student crazy—he will annoy, poke fun, send him or her on meaningless tasks, and do whatever he can to piss off the mentee. Mollie is *your* spiritual teacher. Whenever she gets under your skin, causing you to react in anger or impatience or simply pulls you away from a state of peace, she's showing you exactly where you need to work on yourself." John finished by posing the magical question of the day: "Understand?"

I was in awe. John's insight was more like a full-blown epiphany than simply "understanding" something. After two hours with him, my hyperactive mind had relaxed, and his message was now crystal clear. It especially rang true as I reflected on my approach to writing the new book. Scribbling in my journal, I wrote: "If I am going to write about Mollie, I must first understand her. Understanding her nature (the daily habits that allow her to love everyone) will lead to wisdom. Wisdom then leads to action. And taking action will create the results I desire—enlightenment through unconditional love."

Simply put, before I could authentically teach others her four-legged approach to enlightenment, I had to experience it for myself. I decided right then and there that not only was I going to write about Mollie's wisdom, *I was going to live it.*

On the drive home, my mind replayed everything John had told me. It all made sense. His insight was particularly relevant that day, since I was angry with a few people in my life. It was now clear that they, too, were my spiritual teachers, revealing the places within myself that needed work. In addition to now seeing Mollie as a guru, I also understood what my Buddhist friend meant that morning when he said, "Everything and everyone is a practice—the good, the bad, even the extremely ugly. Anything sent your way only exists to move you closer to enlightenment." After thinking about this philosophical point of view, I realized that his lesson wasn't just about me. It applied to *everyone.* Even Mollie! The challenges that she has faced in her life were a part of her own spiritual curriculum.

One of the first things you notice about Mollie is that despite her adverse experiences, she has apparently not wasted her life thinking about the past, especially the first eight weeks of her life. Clearly, they weren't easy. Some might even say that she had an abusive childhood. Yet anyone who meets Mollie for the first time can only assume that a sweet old couple must have bred her on a farm surrounded by a golden field filled with dog treats. But why think otherwise? She's constantly bouncing off of the walls and grateful to be alive! She sees each day as an exciting new adventure that's filled with endless opportunities. Mollie has no interest whatsoever in reliving her past. She got over it, moved on, and has chosen to embrace the here-and-now. And because there are walks to take, people to kiss, cats to chase, and the bliss of afternoon naps, why be anything but happy? My dog really gets it: each moment of life is a gift.

Everyone has a story to tell. But for some, their personal history actually becomes a leash that holds them back from experiencing life to the fullest. Playing the victim card will never allow them to love unconditionally or achieve enlightenment. That being said, letting go of the past doesn't mean that we need to deny our experiences. As my friend John wisely stated, whatever life throws our way is *for* us, not against us. Rather than use our minds as emotionally draining time machines, we can instead view the past with appreciation for all it has taught us. By acknowledging our challenges as vehicles for spiritual growth, we can transform self-pity into self-love. This perspective also helps us to develop more compassion toward others who may be in similar circumstances.

A heartwarming example of this was recently shown on the evening news. The story was about Hopalong Cassidy IV, a golden retriever born without a front-right paw. His owner, Bernadette "Bernie" Ponzio, adopted Hopalong from a small animal clinic after his breeder called him "worthless" because she couldn't get any money for him. Ponzio stated that the breeder had even planned to put down the disabled dog.

Now more than two years old and using a prosthetic leg, the dog has mastered the art of walking, inspiring people wherever he goes. Ponzio, who was the first of nine people wanting to adopt the puppy, has trained him to become a therapy dog. She brings him to schools as a way of encouraging students to look beyond physical disabilities.

Perhaps the most touching part of this story was seeing Gage Oakley, a high-school senior, gently caress Hopalong's smooth coat when he visited. Gage was diagnosed with osteosarcoma and lost his left leg. This courageous young man, who also has a prosthetic leg, said, "Seeing man's best friend deal with a similar struggle means a lot. I know I'm not the only one out there like that." The touching news piece ends by showing Gage and his new friend walking side by side down the school halls.

No one is immune to life's difficulties. They're simply a part of our existence. Stories such as this one are powerful reminders that using our challenges as a way to serve others is the key to turning suffering into joy. Understanding this truth is not only vital to making peace with oneself, it also brings us a step closer to loving everyone.

My friend John was right . . . it all begins with *understanding*.

Chapter 8

Simple Reminders

When I decided to embark on a quest for the secrets to inner peace and unconditional love by way of Mollie, I'll admit I was unsure how it would all play out. The truth is that it seemed a little crazy at first. But ever since beginning this new journey, I've made a few rather surprising discoveries. Some were major awakenings, while others have been gentle taps on the head, reminding me of forgotten spiritual truths that I learned long ago.

Interestingly enough, during my presentations I often tell my audiences, "There is nothing new I can teach you here today. The only thing I can do is *remind* you of what you already know in your heart to be true." As a whole, my lectures and workshops are stating the obvious. Most people know that being kinder to others, the earth, and themselves is the right thing to do. That being said, some don't live this way, and instead spend their days unaware of their actions. I suggest, "Think of this presentation as a jump start for your heart—I am only here to awaken a part of you that may have dozed off."

Mollie has been a much-needed jolt to my system, reminding me of the best way to live. To my amazement, most of her teachings have been quite simple. I sometimes get caught in the trap of thinking that spirituality has to be a deep, philosophical path, and that transforming my life is something that will take a lifetime of study and meditation. Lately, I am beginning to think that I've had it all wrong. Perhaps major changes in life have no room for complexity.

Just recently, while attending a charity function, I met a woman who exemplified radical transformation through simplicity. As we were waiting for the festivities of the night to begin, she looked my way and posed the most commonly asked question when meeting someone new: "So, what do you do?"

After telling her that I was a writer and a speaker in the self-help field, she said, "Oh, I've heard those books are very good for people! I'd love to read one someday." Her attitude and vibrant spirit made it seem as if she must have already read several books on positive thinking. We discussed my vocation for a minute or two, and then I asked her to tell me a little about herself. She immediately responded with pride, "Well, my name is Mary, I'm 64, and I just retired!"

I was shocked. This woman didn't look one bit over 50. Her huge smile and vivacious energy took years off of her age. "Wow! You do not look old enough to be retired," I said.

"How old did you think I was?" she asked, now glowing. I decided to make her night.

"Forty-eight . . . maybe forty-nine."

She laughed at my kindness and threw her arms around me.

After releasing me from her bear hug, Mary continued, "If you'd seen me a year ago, you probably wouldn't have thought I was that young. I've made some *big* changes!"

I quickly scanned her face, uncertain of what she meant. I tried not to make my first thought obvious: *Oh, she must have had some work done.* But her skin and facial features looked very natural to me. Either she had an amazing plastic surgeon, or I was totally clueless.

Seeing my eyes roam across her face, she smiled widely and corrected me: "Not my face, silly, my body!" I froze. My own facial features began to change, as I felt my cheeks turn as red as a cooked lobster. *Oh . . . she had that kind of work done.* But I was smart enough to keep my mouth shut. Even if my wife hadn't been three feet away, I wasn't about to comment on her "retirement gifts"! Finally, she let me off the hook. Throwing her arms into the air, she did a Rocky-Balboa-like pose and exclaimed, "I lost 85 pounds!"

I could feel my skin tone return to its normal shade as I silently said, *Thank God she didn't mean the "changes" I thought she was talking about!*

Then I enthusiastically replied, "That's amazing! How long did it take you to do that?"

Looking back at me in a casual, it's-no-big-deal way, she said, "A little less than a year." I had total admiration for her. Just losing my "winter weight" each spring always feels like a daunting task.

The big question on my mind now was *how?* How had Mary been able to accomplish this incredible feat? I assumed a program such as Jenny Craig or Weight Watchers must have been a part of her radical transformation. Or perhaps it was a strict no-carb diet, a juice cleanse, or an intense gym routine. But rather than make the same mistake twice through the deadly trap of assumption, this time I asked, "What's your secret?"

With her head held high and shoulders back, she smiled and proudly explained, "I stopped eating crap and started moving more."

This answer seemed way too simple, even unrealistic, so I inquired again. "Oh, come on. What else did you do?"

Her body language remained confident as she enthusiastically responded, "Nothing! I just gave up unhealthy food, turned off the TV, and walked a few miles each evening. That's it!"

My discussion with Mary reminded me just how important good health is in the art of loving everyone. Canine or human, the physical form is the primary way we maneuver through life to express love. It's simple: if we feel good, we do good. Mary's success even encouraged me to look at Mollie's approach to wellness, and I now apply four of her canine habits into my daily routine in my effort to duplicate her feel-good ways: 1) get adequate rest and take power naps, 2) make water my primary drink, 3) have portion control at mealtime, and 4) make exercise and play a daily part of life. It all may sound very basic, but Mollie's health regimens have resulted in higher energy and lower weight for both of us—a significant reminder that tiny changes can have profound, lasting effects.

As I write these words, I am reflecting on a whole new perspective to understanding Mollie's heart. All along I've been thinking that there must be more to her abilities of being nonjudgmental and expressing love for all beings. Each day I have been looking for the big answers. But maybe there isn't "more" to it . . . but rather, *less*. The words of Henry David Thoreau come to mind: "Our life is frittered away by detail. Simplify, simplify, simplify! I say, let your affairs be as two or three, and not a hundred or a thousand; instead of a million count half a dozen, and keep your accounts on your thumb-nail."

Toward the end of my photography career, I learned this valuable lesson from Darton Drake, a master photographer from Baraboo, Wisconsin. His skills as a portrait artist are world renowned. He also happens to be the epitome of cool. The teachings of this Harley-riding, cigar-smoking, camera-toting guru took my photography career to a whole new level. After just one week of studying with him, my uninspiring portraits were revolutionized into soulful pieces of artwork. Although Darton had 30-plus years of photographic knowledge to draw upon, he made it clear that there was just one rule he wanted me to follow. I'll never forget his wise words: "As an artist, you only need to know one thing: simplicity is power." His advice changed not only my photography career, but also my perspective on life. He taught me that stripping away unnecessary clutter and complexities reveals the true spirit.

Simplicity appears to be a key reason why Mollie lives and loves in the moment. As I look around the room, I can see that her material life could fit inside of a small box—water and food dishes, two leashes, one soccer ball, three stuffed toys, two bones to keep her teeth clean, a homemade quilt, and her only outfit: a pink and blue collar. Talk about traveling light! I realize that she's a dog, but there's still wisdom here—wisdom that leads to love. Fourteenth-century mystic Meister Eckehart said it best: "The spiritual life is not a process of addition, but rather of subtraction."

When Cara and I recently watched our material life disappear, we were initially devastated. Our home and other large items were the first to vanish. Then came the "everything must go" sale. Total strangers with crumpled-up dollar bills arrived in our yard one by one, getting the deals of a lifetime on clothes, furniture, holiday decorations, tools, lawn mowers, bikes, and kitchenware. We needed cash, but also had to lighten our load because we were moving—moving, mind you, back to the *exact* place we'd lived ten years before buying our home: to our friend's tiny attic apartment on the third floor of his house.

At first, this took some getting used to. But it wasn't long before we recognized the incredible benefits of our new life. When we owned a home, our weekends were spent cutting the lawn, gardening, raking, cleaning gutters, or chipping away at the endless home improvements on our to-do list. And that was only the summertime! Winter always created a frozen battleground that entailed shoveling, snow blowing, clearing the roof of snow, and salting to keep us from falling on icy stairs.

We've since rediscovered the freedom that comes from a life of simplicity. Now, rather than investing all of our time in household chores, we have the liberty to invest in something far more vital: each other. Instead of maintaining a house (and stressing about a large mortgage payment), we now pedal our bikes, take long walks with Mollie on the beach, or relax and read books. Living by a less-is-more philosophy has given us the gift of time, and, more important, strengthened our relationship.

Most spiritual teachers will tell you that less stuff equals a quieter mind, heightened awareness, and an open heart. In my search for enlightenment, I sometimes forget just how transformative simplicity can be. But each day Mollie is reminding me that living with less allows the much-needed space for doing inner work and cultivating loving relationships. Even right now, as I look down where she is sitting to my left, the contentment in her eyes appears to be telling me, *Everything you need is right here, right now. To be authentically happy, know when enough is enough and live from that place.*

For me, in this very moment, just having Mollie by my side is more than enough.

Chapter 9

Wag More, Bark Less

I despise trash day. Everything about it stinks. Not only does the smell of garbage baking in the morning sun turn my stomach, but it also makes walking Mollie pure hell. With each heap we pass, her nose pulsates as if she's hot on the trail of a cat that has been dipped in peanut butter. We walk in the street, hugging the curb to avoid the piles of bags on the sidewalks. Unfortunately, this strategy is often thwarted by the wet trail of nastiness that has been dripping from the rear of the garbage truck. Once Mollie gets a whiff of this delightful liquid potpourri, it's off to the races and into the road—she's bobbing, weaving, and pulling me every which way but loose. These are the days people sarcastically yell at us from across the street, "Hey, who's walking whom?"

When it comes to my feelings about trash day, I'm not alone. Others hate it, too. But for them, it's much worse; it means war. They fight something far more aggressive than a garbage-sniffing poodle. This is especially true for those who have opted out of trash cans and have instead chosen to leave over-stuffed bags at the ends of their driveways. Living seven miles from the ocean, this is an unwise deci-sion. Just this morning, I witnessed a fierce encoun-ter. *Pop! Pop! Pop!* Shots were fired, an aerial attack ensued, whitish-gray bombs fell from the sky, and curse words ricocheted throughout the neighbor-hood. For a brief moment, my neighbor was under the illusion that he had won this epic battle. But no sooner had he put down his Red Ryder BB Gun . . . when the enemy returned. They are relentless, the vilest of all trash-picking varmints: *seagulls*.

I don't own a high-powered air rifle, or any weapons for that matter. So, if seagulls have spread their good fortune into the roads, my only defense is a custom-made, two-foot canvas strap—a short leash. Surviving a walk with Mollie on trash day all comes down to keeping her nose up and her eyes straight ahead. If her muzzle is allowed to touch the ground, she'll invariably find a way to consume a second, third, or, if she's really quick, a fourth morning meal. Of course, her idea of breakfast is not always something you and I would order from our favorite diner. On occasion, she lucks out and the crust of someone's toast or a long-lost crouton may present itself, but more often than not, it's a greasy napkin that she inhales—a perfect complement to the bowl of Parmesan cheese–covered kibble she just ate at home.

Although my BB-gun-toting neighbor would likely disagree, my trash-day scuffles are far more dangerous than his. He's never been pulled into oncoming traffic for an empty donut bag. Nor has he ever attempted to pry items out of clenched canine teeth. (This task is a hazardous one, to say the least, and I have the scars to prove it!)

Just last week, Mollie and I were heading through a garbage-and-gull war zone, as I weaved around the shredded two-ply bags like a pro. I was doing everything I was supposed to do: keeping her leash high and tight and walking a wide circle around the debris. I even talked to her, which is my way of keeping her focused on me and not on the eggshells, potato peelings, and half-eaten cream puffs. But then something went drastically wrong. I blinked or simply placed my focus where it didn't belong; whatever the reason, I hadn't seen what was in our path. But

Mollie had. And in one powerful lunge, she reached down just far enough to suck up the mother of all trash treats.

"Oh, come on, Mollie!" I said under my breath. *Crunch.* I had no idea what she'd found, but if there were such a thing as a crunch meter, on a scale of one to ten Mollie's new treasure would have been a solid eight. Grabbing onto her snout, I then tried to reason with her. "Why . . . *why* do you do this?" *Crunch. Crunch.* With my other hand, I began the all-too-familiar process of digging through her mouth. *Chips,* I thought. *They must be homemade potato chips.* It only made sense after seeing the mound of potato peelings a few yards back. But as my fingers slid into her throat, I soon realized that Mollie had hit the jackpot. She'd found the most sought after of all garbage delicacies: chicken bones!

Mollie chomped away at the now-shredded, teriyaki-flavored splinters in hopes of swallowing the bones before I could get them out of her mouth. Shoving my fingers down her throat, I was able to get a good grip. I pulled, plucked, and then flung the slimy shards to the ground. There were still tiny pieces to remove, but I was mostly concerned about the drumstick lodged deep below her tongue. Wrapping my fingers around it, I began to tug . . . and that's when the crunch meter went from an 8 to a 108. Mollie clamped down onto the chicken bone, splitting it in two, which sent its pointy end into my finger like a hot knife through butter. Ripping my hand from her jaws, I screamed in pain. Seconds later, my blood-soaked finger matched the color of the KFC box lying on the ground behind us. It was as if Colonel Sanders had just stabbed me.

I was fuming. I knew it wasn't Mollie's fault— she would never intentionally hurt me—but this was *not* how I wanted to start my day. As I wrapped my blood-soaked hand in an empty poop bag, we started our long walk back home. With each step, I felt a fiery anger building inside of me. People soon began to stare at me with my hand wrapped in a bag and bloodstained cargo shorts. The inner child in me felt like blurting out, "Why don't you take a picture? It will last longer!" I became even more annoyed when they gawked at Mollie's social-media-worthy act of puking up her original breakfast, now fresh with chicken-bone remnants. *Tweet this,* I thought.

I was now in a full-blown state of fury. Everything was making me mad, especially people's "trash" items. Each time we'd pass a home that had tin cans, cardboard, newspapers, and other such items thrown curbside, I felt like knocking on the door and saying,

"Hey, there's a new thing we're doing here on Earth; it's called recycling. Have you heard of it?" Walking past another home, I seethed even more upon seeing garbage strewn across the road by seagulls. This mess was the result of the homeowners leaving their bags on the sidewalk without any protection. I then began to hypothesize about what I assumed they spent their money on instead of buying a trash can. I noticed two empty cardboard boxes—one from an air conditioner and the other from an empty case of beer. Irate thoughts popped into my mind. *If you can afford cold air and some cold Buds, you sure as hell can afford a trash can!* I was on a tear.

Taking a shortcut through a shopping plaza, I stumbled across two kids rocking a vending machine back and forth. It was obvious that these soda bandits were attempting to steal whatever sugary drinks lay inside. I stopped, turned, and glared back at them through my dark sunglasses as if I were Arnold Schwarzenegger in *The Terminator*—stone-faced and bloody. They ran. Watching these delinquents scurry across the parking lot, I thought, *My school presentations aren't making a difference. Kids today don't care. They're so disrespectful.* With only five minutes left of our journey home, Mollie jabbed her nose into my side pocket, which held her dog treats. I handed her a cookie, and then noticed a familiar figure walking toward us. I've seen this man on many occasions while driving around town. He walks everywhere. With each step he takes, his messy, shoulder-length hair bounces as if it has a life of its own. His swinging arms and powerful momentum keep people on edge. But what makes him appear even more unusual is the way he carries on conversations with himself. On most days, he's looking up, conversing with the sky. His words are intense and always seem quite important.

I considered crossing the street to avoid him, but instead decided to put my head down and continue moving forward. Now, with only 20 yards between us, I cinched Mollie's leash up tight to my side to keep her from greeting this man. Looking down at her, I immediately noticed that something was wrong with this picture, and I'm not sure if I was more shocked or insulted by what I saw. It just didn't seem right—her ears were perked up, her tail was wagging, and, as usual, she maintained her goofy grin. Simply put, *Mollie looked happy.* This seemed like blasphemy! Between the chicken-bone episode, trash blowing in the streets, my dog vomiting in public, soda-stealing teenagers, irresponsible people who don't recycle, and now a guy who appeared to be a few French fries short of a Happy Meal, there was *no* reason to be happy whatsoever!

But she was. As a matter of fact, she looked ecstatic.

I then realized that I'd been walking home alone. Mollie may have been by my side physically, but energetically speaking we were on different planets. All of my pissing and moaning, all of my complaining, all of my judgment toward others was *my* stuff. Even though we'd both experienced the same events that morning, she chose to enjoy the walk . . . and I chose to be completely miserable.

This realization reminded me of what my friend John had taught me during our last meeting. In an effort to help me better understand the Buddhist path, he'd said, "Everything is emptiness. What you see before you only has meaning because of the labels you place on it."

He then removed a pen from his pocket and asked, "What's this?"

Hoping it wasn't a trick question, I answered with hesitancy, "Uh . . . a pen?"

John nodded in agreement. He continued, "And what is it used for?"

Feeling more confident this time, I quickly replied, "You write with it."

Again, he looked at me as if to say that I was correct.

Next, he did something that I wasn't expecting. Lifting the pen to his mouth, he began to aggressively chomp on it with his teeth. I could see in my peripheral vision that people sitting in the booth beside us glanced our way. He then asked, "In Mollie's eyes, what is this?"

It became apparent that there was a deeper lesson to be learned here, but seeing the pen clamped between his teeth I chose the most obvious answer: "A chew toy?"

"Exactly!" John replied. He went on, "It's only a pen based on the label we place on it with our minds. It means something different to everyone. If the pen was on the ground, an ant would see it as a major obstacle to walk around."

So cool, I thought.

He finished by adding, "Nothing has a nature of its own. Everything that exists is only manifested through our perceptions."

John's message now rang true—whether it's people or smelly trash, my negative attitude would never define who or what is in front of me. It only defines me as an angry, opinionated, judgmental, and trash-hating *you know what*. Unfortunately, I hadn't remembered this truth before setting out with Mollie that morning. But as the Buddha once said, "No matter how hard the past, one can always begin again today."

Looking up, I realized that in seconds we were going to cross paths with a man most of the town had written off as crazy. Clearly, Mollie didn't feel this way. Seeing him approach caused her to be jubilant, not judgmental. The closer we got, the faster her tail swished back and forth through the air. His wild hair, scraggly beard, and even the conversation he was having with himself didn't put her off at all.

With as much positive energy as I could muster up, I exclaimed, "Hey there, good morning!"

Startled by my words, the man immediately ended his conversation with the sky. Pushing the blond hair from his face, he looked at me in awe. I saw no indication of "crazy" in his eyes. Instead, I saw loneliness. His expression told me that he wasn't used to people acknowledging him. With half a smile, he pushed through his speech impediment and returned my greeting. "Hello! Yesss . . . it is a good morning! . . . I hope you have a very nice day!"

I cannot recall ever hearing those words delivered with such sincerity. He didn't just say, "Have a nice day," *he meant it.* And I felt it. Not only did I feel it, but his friendly disposition also hit the reset button in my heart, erasing the effect of the previous half hour in less than three seconds.

The mind is like a giant label maker with two switches, positive and negative. Understanding this, I try to remember that what I consider to be garbage, bears and raccoons see as dinner, seagulls view as a buffet, and city workers look at as job security. Do I love trash day now? Not particularly. But rather than curse it or worry about people's recycling habits, I now know that I have a choice: to be like Mollie, wagging and appreciating what the day has to offer, or to depreciate it by complaining. I must say that focusing on what's right with the world always feels better than grumbling about what's wrong.

And as for my new friend, I now wave to him whenever I see him on the streets. I also have a whole new perspective of him, especially how I view his daily conversations with the sky. The way I see it, he and the man upstairs must be pretty tight.

Chapter 10

Go with the Flow

L ao-tzu, the Chinese master who lived more than 2,500 years ago, authored one of history's most renowned texts called the Tao Te Ching. Often referred to as simply *the Tao,* this spiritual classic offers 81 brief lessons that point toward higher truths and create a deeper understanding of life. *Tao,* pronounced *dow* and meaning "the great way," is considered to be a natural force running through all living and nonliving things that balances, guides, assembles, and connects them. Taoists believe this energy to be the ultimate creative principle of the Universe.

When my brother-in-law Mike first introduced me to the Tao, I wasn't sure it was for me. But after taking his advice and reading it one afternoon, I was hooked. It was like opening 81 fortune cookies, each one holding a message leading to enlightenment. The Tao's teachings are simple, heart opening, often paradoxical, and yet in the end spiritually illuminating.

Lao-tzu's wisdom continues to influence millions of lives to this day. His soothing, poetic words are especially helpful in today's chaotic world. On many occasions, reading them has become a form of meditation for me. But it wasn't until recently that I began to see the Tao through new eyes. While sitting with Mollie, it dawned on me: perhaps Lao-tzu gained his insights by living with a crazy dog, too! Okay, so that's probably not true—actually, he's often shown riding an ox—but there's no denying some of the similarities between his 2,500-year-old philosophy and my four-legged guru's lessons. I'm fully aware that there's a vast difference between a disobedient poodle and ancient Chinese wisdom; however, after years of reflecting on the Tao, I can see how many of its teachings parallel Mollie's approach to life: simplicity, spontaneity, nonjudgment, continual giving, surrendering to what is, resistance to conflict, freedom from the material world, compassion, intuition, living in the present moment, and of course love.

I certainly don't claim to be an authority on the Tao Te Ching or Taoism in general. But after a lay study of Lao-tzu's 81 compositions, I've come to believe that it can be summed up in one sentence: *Go with the flow.* In other words, rather than try to control every situation or push life around like a school-yard bully, the more fruitful alternative is to appreciate it, lean into it, and become one with all that exists. Lao-tzu reminds us that honoring and emulating nature is the path toward inner peace and global harmony. To live in accord with the undeniable beauty of the natural world is to merge into the essence of Tao/God/the Universe, all of which are love.

Regardless of one's religion or belief system, having reverence for all beings just seems like the right thing to do. For me, becoming a vegetarian five years ago was one way I felt I could begin this journey (although I admit that the smell of a barbecue still gets me every time). In addition to this lifestyle change, I also decided to honor and respect all living creatures. Spiders, flies, blood-sucking mosquitoes, mice that live in the cellar, and other so-called nuisances were now caught and released rather than sent to their death. Once, I even escorted, in my opinion, the *nastiest* of all creatures back into the woods—a tick!

Mollie also shows compassion. She's my bug detector, often finding a spider or confused ant scurrying across the floor. Once she spots an insect, she continues to follow it wherever it goes, never once attempting to harm it. I then use my critter catcher, a thin slice of cardboard, to lift and usher our little friends back outside. I'll admit that this is a bit unusual. And, to be honest, things with more than four legs do creep me out. But who am I to decide the fate of any living being? Just because something makes me uncomfortable doesn't give me the right to step on it. And if I do, it's only a reflection of my own fears and insecurities, or, even worse, my contribution to an already-violent world.

Not long ago, Mollie and I started another practice in our effort to appreciate the natural world, one that has definitely turned a few heads. It all began one morning following an evening rainstorm. We were out walking, when I began to notice something on the ground. Worms. They were everywhere. At first, we simply did our best not to step on them. But it wasn't long before I realized that they were potentially crawling to their deaths by slowly dragging their bodies right into the road. It was suicide! Looking down, I saw one struggling; it was clearly going to take him forever and a day to make it to his destination. I felt compassion but kept walking. Twenty feet later, my conscience caught up with me and tapped me on the shoulder. I turned around.

Bending down, I used my fingers to gently pluck the noodlelike creature from the wet asphalt. It twisted and turned, but for the most part didn't resist my offer to give it a lift. Holding the worm in my hand thrust me back to my childhood, a time when worms seemed like an important, even necessary, part of life. It was hard to believe that 30 years prior I was grasping the same living things, only under very different circumstances. Instead of saving them, I was piercing their hearts with razor-sharp hooks and feeding them to fish! Now, looking at this little guy, I felt remorse for dangling his ancestors into the mouths of hungry predators and hoped my new intention would clear away any old karma.

Mollie and I continued this mission, and one by one transported each worm we found from the road onto the lawns of strangers. At one point, a man pulled into his driveway only to catch me placing a giant night crawler underneath his tree. Rather than explain myself, I waved, Mollie wagged, and we quickly scurried away. A mile into our walk, I was presented with an interesting predicament, and, if I was willing, an opportunity to wipe the slate clean from my childhood fishing trips. As we rounded a corner, we saw large puddles that overtook the street. I began to notice that the number of worms was greatly increasing. I had been seeing three or four per road, but here there were at least a dozen. And waiting for us around the next bend was something straight out of a scene from a horror movie.

There must have been over 100 of these slippery, slimy earthworms trying to cross the flooded terrain. The well-groomed field to my right appeared to be their destination. Sadly, many didn't make it. Wet tire tracks offered ample evidence for the invertebrate CSI to go on. Of course, I felt bad seeing the plight of these little guys, but I also realized that saving every one of them wasn't realistic. It reminded me of the sweet story that makes this exact point and is so often repeated:

A little boy was tossing starfish into the ocean as he walked along the shore. Without his act of kindness, they'd have surely baked in the hot sun and died.

Upon seeing his actions, a man yelled over the sound of crashing waves, "Son, don't waste your time! There are hundreds of them. You're not going to make a difference!"

Plucking another starfish from the sand, the young boy tossed it through the salty air into the sea. Looking back at the man, he smiled and said with pride, "It sure made a difference to that one!"

Shortly after I became an advocate for earthworms, Cara joined Mollie and me for a morning walk, and it wasn't long before the first worm made an appearance. As it writhed about, smack-dab in the middle of the road, it became obvious that I had to act fast. Knowing a car could drive toward us at any moment, I swooped in, picked up the worm, offered it a blessing, and then placed it on the lawn to our right, which was about ten feet away.

I felt divinely connected, perhaps even a bit righteous. Not only had I spared the worm's life, I had also taken hours off its commute. I was a hero! That is, until my always-perceptive wife looked at me and said, "How do you know the worm was actually going *that* way?" as she pointed to the right.

I didn't.

As the Tao reminds us, sometimes we simply need to let nature run its course, or like The Beatles told us, just *let it be.* In other words, trying to control or interfere with the inevitable is not our job.

But here's where it gets even more interesting. In my efforts to determine the worm's destiny, I was also doing the same thing it was doing—*hanging out in the middle of the street!* Maybe the real lesson here is to stay the hell out of the way!

Thinking about this, I decided to work on my own control issues, starting with my relationship with Mollie. For example, whenever I attempt to manage her behavior with force, it never works. Pulling on her leash creates stress, using my firm voice instills fear, and bribing her with Scooby Snacks only leads to an unauthentic relationship. None of this is done with love.

So I tried a new approach. *Bock!* Somewhere around 3:00 P.M. on the same day, Mollie informed me that it was time to get up from my writing desk to stretch and, more important, take her out to pee. As usual, she began with her customary chickenlike noise: *Bock!*

I responded with, "Just a minute." But that was a lie; it would be at least five.

Bock! Bock!

"Hold on, Mollie. I'm almost done." But that was a lie, too. I was still online, searching for my favorite Lao-tzu quotes.

Bock. Bock! Bock!! Bock!!! Bock!!!! (Which means, "I have to pee now!")

"Okay, fine!"

With the leash now snapped onto her collar, we ventured down the stairs and into the backyard. As the fresh air hit me in the face, I realized that sitting in the apartment for hours had robbed my senses of the beautiful day. Once in the yard, Mollie always walks straight to her designated pee spot, squats, and within seconds is done. But on this day, I was ready to run back upstairs, while she was not.

I was loosely holding the leash as I walked across the lawn, intending to go back inside. Suddenly, my arm shot straight back, jerked my body around, and brought my momentum to a halt. As I turned, I could see that *someone* wasn't ready to go in the house. But I was. "Not right now, Mollie; we'll come back out later."

She dug in. Her front paws sank deep into the grass, while her butt was planted firmly on the ground. Feeling the pressure to finish my writing and send it to my editor, I was determined to get back to my desk. So I pulled again as I said a little louder this time, "Let's go!"

Deadweight.

There have been times that, rather than play tug-of-war, I'll scoop Mollie off the ground and carry her up the three flights of stairs. It's a ridiculous sight, but that's exactly what I was prepared to do. That is, until I made the very same mistake I'd made eight years prior when choosing between her and another dog—I looked into her eyes. Seeing her pitiful face at the end of the leash melted my impatient heart. She was desperate for a little fresh air. Taking in a deep breath, I sighed and then thought to myself, *Okay . . . practice what you preach . . . go with the flow . . . just go with the flow.* I decided to give Mollie five minutes to enjoy the scenery, and I'd try to do the same.

We're blessed to have a resortlike backyard. The lawn itself is meticulously cut every other day, giving it the look and feel of a golf course. The surrounding gardens are even more impressive. A vibrant array of pink, purple, yellow, red, white, and blue flower species wraps around us like something out of a *Better Homes and Gardens* magazine. To the right sits a small woodworking shop. Santa's elves would be lucky to work there. Quaint lawn furniture is sprinkled in front of it, along with a fire pit, which is perfect for roasting marshmallows at night. There's even a garden cart filled with tomatoes, parsley, oregano, and other herbs used for cooking. And because, like Mollie, I'm spoiled, I haven't lifted a finger to make the yard look this way. It's just one of the huge benefits of renting an apartment from our amazing friends who do all the work.

Kicking off my flip-flops, I began to experience the very sensation Mollie feels each day—the earth under my feet. I cannot believe how connected to nature this made me feel. I even wondered if being barefoot is a spiritual practice worth considering. Mollie then took the lead, guiding me to the right side of the yard where cherry tomatoes grow abundantly—the very ones that grace my salads each day for lunch. She then stopped and began to sniff. The tip of her wet nose kissed every blade of grass in a two-foot radius. On the fence in front of us was a crimson-red cardinal looking our way. I plucked a few tomatoes from the vine and then did something I've never done to a plant before: *expressed gratitude.* I'll admit it; this felt odd at first. I even looked over my shoulder before I allowed the words to escape from my lips. Much to my surprise, whispering "Thank you" to a tomato plant was a blissful experience.

For the next 30 minutes, I followed Mollie everywhere she wanted to go. Releasing my need to control her, and the day, was indescribably freeing. Rather than think about the work waiting for me inside, I was present and in harmony with the gardens—sniffing herbs and touching flowers—and despite neighbors being within earshot, I continued expressing gratitude, thanking each plant for its gifts of food and beauty.

Eventually we made our way back to where I'd left my shoes. This appeared to be Mollie's way of giving me permission to go back inside. Sliding my flip-flops on was like flipping a switch. With my bare feet no longer touching the grass, I was back in work mode, thinking, *I hope I can finish the rest of this chapter today.* Then, Lao-tzu's paradoxical words flashed through my mind: "Nature does not hurry, yet everything is accomplished." Walking up the stairs, I realized that he was right; the chapter was done—in fact, it had practically written itself.

Chapter 11

Into the Light

Some of my fondest memories from when Mollie was a puppy are when we played hide-and-seek in the dark. After the sun fell behind the trees, the squirrels settled down, and Hoppy (the one-legged turkey that occasionally visited our property) ventured back into the woods, it was safe to let Mollie loose. Nighttime always seemed to corral her free-roaming spirit, keeping her within the limits of our yard. There was nothing more thrilling than watching her run free as her lean body raced laps around the house and her eyes sparkled with the joy of a kid on Christmas day.

I would start the game by hurling her soccer ball into the night air. Once it landed near the end of the yard, she'd blast off to retrieve it while I ran to hide. Her speed and determination were incredible. I only had seconds to duck behind a tree, a pile of wood, or, if I was fast enough, roll underneath my truck. Looking out from my hiding spot, I could see her silhouette zip back and forth searching for me, which made my heart pound with elation. Once the ball was recovered and clamped tightly in her jaw, Mollie would bounce from one dark corner of the yard to another, not quitting until she saw me.

If hiding from Mollie was fun, being found was pure bliss! Once I was caught, she barked with delight, hopping on her hind legs while placing both of her front paws squarely on top of my shoulders. You'd think we hadn't seen each other in weeks. I remember playing this game as a young boy. If you were tagged, it meant you lost the game. But having Mollie pull me from the darkness always made me feel as if I was the winner.

Perhaps this is why I've always loved the word *guru*. Descriptions vary, but many claim that a guru gives spiritual guidance, illuminating the path of one's soul from the shadows into the light. Therefore, one who removes darkness from the life of another is considered a guru. In addition to bringing one into the light, it's said that, on a deeper level, these divine spiritual teachers understand their pupils unlike any other. Some students have claimed that their gurus even have the ability to read their thoughts and energy.

In Mollie's case, I've found this to be true. Her intuitive gifts seem supernatural to me. It's as if she knows my thoughts and intentions before I make a move. The mere notion of going for a drive causes her to do a jig. Or, if I simply *feel* like playing toss with her stuffed toy chicken, she'll immediately bring it to me. And then there's peanut butter, her favorite treat, which is occasionally spread onto a dog cookie. She can be in a hibernating state of sleep, but if I go into the kitchen even entertaining the thought of making a PB-and-J sandwich . . . she's at my feet!

I've also begun to notice how her ability to read energy is apparent when someone is experiencing grief or any other form of inner turmoil. Most recently, when I had an emotional school presentation to give, she could tell that something was wrong.

It had been a bittersweet year. On the upside, though, the students at the schools I'd been working with were reacting in extremely positive ways to my program; there had been a noticeable decline in bullying, and now performing acts of kindness was even thought of as cool. On the downside, there had been many tragedies to work through—depression, abusive parents, homelessness, and addiction. This week, a young girl at a local high school had committed suicide, and I'd soon be speaking to over 800 teens, hoping to be a part of their healing process.

While I was doing yoga that morning before the presentation, Mollie visited my mat, stretched, did her own downward-dog pose, and then placed her body right up against mine. Looking up at me with compassion, her eyes appeared to say, "What's wrong, Daddy?" I rolled to my side and gently pulled her close. With my arms around her, I buried my nose into her soft coat and closed my eyes. For the next several minutes, we did nothing but breathe simultaneously. With each breath she took in, I followed. When she exhaled, I did the same. It was a rhythmic dance. Feeling her heartbeat against my chest also kept me centered and relieved the anxiety I was feeling about the upcoming day. Although this meditation was brief, its effects were lasting.

Despite shedding a few tears that day and breaking the no-hugging policy over 100 times, it was perhaps the best talk I'd ever given at a school. What was supposed to be only an hour turned into much more. After my presentation, the principal asked me to stay for the day to work one-on-one with several students. Some told me their personal stories, while others wanted to discuss the latest tragedy. The entire day, I made it my intention to offer the students the same gift Mollie had given me: loving presence. She had taught me the most sought-after of all spiritual traits: to be completely immersed in the here-and-now.

Sadly, we're living in a time where the ability to stay present with those in front of us has become a foreign concept. Eyes are continually looking down and fingers are ablaze posting, tweeting, texting, e-mailing, and chatting. Technology is truly amazing in the way it connects people, but it's also having the opposite effect at times, keeping us disconnected from each other. I can recall many instances of talking with someone, even baring my soul, only to have his or her next incoming message take precedence over me. I've been guilty of this, too. I'm ashamed to say that, on occasion, I've pretended that there's something of the utmost importance on my phone while in the midst of an uncomfortable social situation. It seems that to look down is the easiest way to armor the heart. I'm a big fan of technology, and

I'm grateful for the many ways it enhances my life. But personally speaking, there have been too many times when it has kept me in the dark and even stolen my natural state of awareness.

Thich Nhat Hanh has been an inspiration to me. He said, "The most precious gift we can offer others is our presence. When our mindfulness embraces those we love, they will bloom like flowers." His wise teachings have led me toward more silence and deeper meditation, especially a walking meditation. Not only has this practice heightened my awareness, but it has also strengthened my bond with Mollie. In fact, I noticed its benefits the first time I tried it. As we were walking, I slowed my pace and began to recall Hanh's instruction to "Practice conscious breathing by counting steps." With each step I took, I attempted to become more aware of my breath. The first minute or so I felt somewhat clumsy, even concerned that I might walk into a telephone pole. But after getting a rhythm going, it was surprisingly easy. Breath, step, step, breath, step, step, breath, and so on. As we sped up a bit, I heard the perfect sound to focus on—the click, click, click of Mollie's nails making contact with the asphalt. So I switched my concentration from my own steps to hers. This immersed me even further into the moment, allowing me to experience things that I'd never fully noticed before: the sensation of a breeze, the warmth of the sun on the back of my neck, birds singing, and even the smell of coffee brewing as I walked past several homes.

Over and over, Mollie has shown me that loving others is only possible if we're fully present. Whenever I've needed the comfort of a friend, her company and full attention have been my saving grace. And even though she may not be able to verbalize how much she cares, she's always there by my side, in good times and bad, pulling me out of the darkness and into the light.

While giving a workshop at a Hay House I Can Do It! conference, I met a woman whose story illustrates this point. I had picked Ann out of the crowd to be a volunteer for an exercise I was doing. Following my presentation, she approached me with tears in her eyes, wanting to share more of her personal story. After hearing it, I asked Ann if she would write it down so it could be shared with the world.

And so she did:

In July of 1994, we added a beautiful golden-retriever puppy to our family, and my son named her Simba. I should have realized the fact that she was born on my birthday was more than just a co-incidence. She was the most loving and happy dog you'd ever meet. My son would roll around and pull on her, and she never so much as groaned. All of my nieces and nephews loved Simba, and she loved them, too. She was a member of our family.

Over the course of the next 12 years, my husband and I had fertility issues trying to conceive and have another child. I started drinking to drown my sorrows. As the months passed, the cunning, baffling, and very powerful disease of alcoholism was slowly winning the battle inside me; and I was in serious denial. Simba was always by my side; she was the only one who knew all my secrets and lies. I would lie with her and cry my eyes out, asking myself, *Why can't I stop drinking?* She would gently kiss my face; she loved me no matter what. I could see the love and genuine concern in her eyes when I would drink. I felt she was the only one who truly knew my pain and self-loathing. In my last year of drinking, she developed a cancerous tumor on her back leg. I couldn't stand the thought of losing her . . . she was my best friend.

In the summer of 2006, as the saying goes, I hit rock bottom. My husband gave me an ultimatum. My drinking was starting to affect our 15-year-old son—my one and only child whom

I desperately loved—so I agreed to go to 28-day inpatient rehab at Father Martin's Ashley. On the day I left the house, I asked Simba to please try to hold on until I returned home. She was getting weaker, but she walked to the door wagging her tail and kissed me good-bye.

Father Martin's Ashley saved my life. When my husband and son returned the next weekend to visit me, I couldn't wait to see them. I felt so alive being one week sober. My husband told me that Simba wasn't doing well, and he thought that it was "her time." From the day I left for rehab, he said that she'd barely eaten and was having difficulty getting around. I was so sad, but I knew it wouldn't be fair to make her suffer until I came home. I desperately wanted to be there when she was put to sleep. My counselors didn't think it would be a good idea for me to leave the facility, so my dear husband brought Simba to me so I could say good-bye. I held Simba and cried . . . but I made her a promise that I vowed to keep. "Simba, it's okay, honey, for you to go to heaven. Your job here is done. I promise you, Mommy is getting better and will never drink again."

When they left, I walked around the grounds and noticed for the first time that there were three flat gravestones on the lawn overlooking the water. They had sayings on them that seemed as if they were for dogs. After inquiring, I found out that Father Martin had three golden retrievers during his life, and they were all buried here. I smiled and felt such hope. Looking up, I told Simba to have fun running around in heaven with Father Martin's dogs.

Simba was far more than my dog . . . she was my angel. And when I promised her that I was getting better, I meant it. I've been sober since that day and will be celebrating six years of sobriety on October 9, 2012. Simba taught me unconditional love and the true meaning of a saying we use in Alcoholics Anonymous: "You have to give it away to keep it."

Chapter 12

Curiosity

It was the perfect morning to be on the pond. The water looked like glass as we drove up to the boat landing, and subtle rays of pink and orange spread throughout the sky as the sun was beginning to break over the horizon. Maine offers many picturesque scenes, but for me the tranquility of a lake or pond at 5 A.M. has always given me a feeling of peace. Floating along the shoreline in a small aluminum boat while sipping coffee is perhaps the most powerful form of meditation I've ever experienced.

After backing the boat into the water, I drove to the parking lot across the street, grabbed a few items from the truck bed, and walked around to open the passenger door. The front window, which had been clean five minutes before, now had a fresh layer of drool and nose prints covering it. From the moment we arrived, Mollie had been bouncing up and down with excitement. Trying to keep her mellow, I held her leash and said, "Okay, girl, calm down."

Walking to the shore's edge, Mollie began cautiously dipping her front paws in the water, and then dropped her snout in as if she could smell the very thing we'd come here for: largemouth bass.

"Do you smell fish, Mol?" Hearing her name, she swung her head back around to look at me. "Fish, girl, we're here to catch some fish!" Her tail wagged back and forth with pure excitement. In reality, though, Mollie had no idea what I was talking about. It was the spring of 2005 and our very first fishing trip together.

When I pushed the boat into the water, Mollie acted excited but at the same time a bit confused. Seeing the land get smaller and farther away appeared to create a moment of anxiety in her. But before long, she became fascinated with the open water. Not wanting to spook her, I decided to let us drift for a few minutes instead of using the motor. Soon, she was hopping from one end of the boat to the other, completely in awe of her new surroundings.

Once we were in deeper water, I began to prepare my rods and favorite lures. Being the queen of curiosity, Mollie immediately stuck her nose into a huge bag of artificial, neon-green worms that I had at my feet. "No, not those, girl. Those are too bright for this water." Reaching into my tackle box, I pulled out another bag and said, "These black-and-blue ones are the color to use on Kennebunk Pond."

We had drifted about 200 yards out and were positioned perfectly in front of a small island I knew well. While out with fishing buddies, I'd discovered this spot between two large rocks that always produced a fish or two. With my preferred lure now tied on, I looked down at Mollie and said, "Okay, are you ready? Let's catch some fish." At the time she was only a year old, and her puppy face smiled back at me, clueless as to what I was doing but just happy to be with me. "Here we go, Mollie!" Pulling the tip of the rod back, I then motioned forward and let it fly. *Wzzzz . . . plunk.* It was one of the prettiest casts I'd ever seen.

The worm had no more than hit the surface when *splash!* The water exploded into the air as a hungry bass engulfed my entire bait. "Yes! Check it out, girl! First cast!" She put both paws on the edge of the boat and began to stare eagerly at the strange activity 40 feet away. Keeping my line tight, I slowly reeled the fish toward us. Occasionally it would break water, shaking its body back and forth, which excited my puppy even more.

With only a few feet of fishing line left in the water, I had to push Mollie back so I could grab our first catch of the day. "Hold on, girl. You'll get to see him. You've got to move back for a second." She wouldn't budge. I tried again, but there was no way she was leaving her spot. Finally, I guided my line to the back of the boat, where only I had access. Submerging my hand into the warm water, I slid my thumb into the two-pounder's mouth, hoisting him into the boat.

"Check it out! This is a fish!" Rushing to my feet, Mollie nearly knocked me over to get a closer look at the foreign creature. Her nose went ballistic. Had I not pulled this bass away, she would have sniffed its scales off. "Okay, Mol, time to let him go. We just catch fish; we don't keep them." As I held the largemouth out over the edge of the boat, Mollie's eyes widened and stared at me as if to say, "Let it go? Are you nuts?" Dipping him gently into the water, I opened my hands as he slowly began to swim away. Mollie looked at me, then the water, then me . . . and that's when she guaranteed that we wouldn't catch another fish in that spot for the rest of the day. *She dove in!*

After seeing the fish glide down to the bottom of the pond, my now fish-crazed dog leaped in, swimming under the boat in an attempt to rescue what had just gotten away.

No, this is not a fish story. When it happened, I was so shocked that I froze. I didn't know if I should dive in after her or grab my camera! It didn't take long before Mollie realized that, unlike her gilled friend, she couldn't breathe underwater. A few seconds later, her head popped up and she began a frantic doggy paddle back to me. Grabbing Mollie under her belly, I lifted her waterlogged body, which nearly capsized us. It took several tries, but eventually I was able to pull her out of the pond as we both collapsed onto the boat floor.

Now I was soaking wet, too. I stood up to see a man on the end of his dock waving and yelling in our direction. "You guys okay?"

Laughing, I replied, "It's the first time she's ever seen a fish. She tends to get excited whenever she sees something new."

After taking a long drag from his cigarette, he replied in his thick Maine accent, "Ayah. Musta been a big un' for her to jump in like that!"

Scott Adams, the creator of the "Dilbert" comic strip, once said, "The first time you see something that you have never seen before, you almost always know right away if you should eat it or run away from it." In Mollie's case, it didn't appear that her interest was in either of those choices. Her zest for life could more accurately be summed up in Eleanor Roosevelt's beautiful words: "I think, at a child's birth, if a mother could ask a fairy godmother to endow it with the most useful gift, that gift would be curiosity."

Whether it's seeing a fish for the first time or someone new walking down the street, looking at life with curiosity appears to be Mollie's remedy for a judgmental mind. The way she views the world with wonder rather than through critical eyes is a practice that I aspire to each day. I consider it to be one of her most spiritual traits and the biggest discovery I've made when trying to understand authentic love. Having an appreciation for all that exists is difficult, but it's a must for anyone in search of inner peace.

Just recently, while on my way to the pet store with Mollie for some dog cookies, I was given several opportunities to work on my openness toward others. Normally it's a short drive from where we live, but construction, combined with the tourist season, had slowed things down that day. Soon the traffic had come to a complete halt. As I sat there waiting to begin moving again, I saw a young woman standing on the sidewalk just a few feet from my car. Glancing up, I noticed her oversized shirt, which was black and covered with images of skulls. I looked at her face, trying not to make my thoughts obvious, and it seemed to me that she'd probably had a rough night. Beneath her eyes were deep, dark circles. This woman must have been sleep deprived for weeks. When she moved closer to my car, my mind began to race, thinking about the likelihood of drugs, alcohol, and God only knows what she'd been doing.

As I continued making my unfair observation, I caught a glance of the strange activity taking place in the backseat of my car. Mollie's head was sticking out the window, tail wagging, desperately wanting to turn another stranger into a friend. You could see the wonder gleaming in her eyes: *Hey, where'd you get that awesome shirt? Do you like to ride in cars, too? I love it! Oh, by the way, I'm Mollie. What's your name?*

Seconds later the traffic began to move, but it wasn't long before we were in gridlock again. Mollie and I had traveled no more than a quarter of a mile, when we found ourselves in the middle of Route 1 parked in front of several run-down buildings. Loiterers often occupied this particular spot; and lately a young man asking for bottles, food, cash, or anything you'd be willing to give had been a regular fixture there. As I casually turned to my left, pretending to look for something in my seat, I could see him on his perch, holding a cigarette in one hand and a cardboard sign in the other.

Please don't misunderstand me; I give to homeless people all the time. But something about this kid didn't seem right. In my mind he was a scammer. I saw greed, not need. He simply didn't exude the qualities I was used to seeing in people who are living on the street. He was young, appeared mentally and physically sound, and, in all honesty, just looked like a lazy kid to me. While sitting in my car only ten feet away, I continued to ignore his presence. But as I'm sure you can guess by now, *you know who* was indifferent to my judgmental attitude. My decision to not offer this young man a couple of bucks hadn't stopped Mollie from giving something even more valuable—love and attention. Just as before, her face was now protruding from the window as if to say, *Hey there! Whatcha doing? Is that where you live? It's a really nice spot! Oh, by the way, I'm Mollie. What's your name?*

We finally made it to our destination. I quickly ran inside, purchased a bag of cookies, and we were soon on our way home. Thankfully, the traffic was much lighter. But as we drove past the building where the kid was sitting, I was pelted with an ego-bruising thought, *Even if I'm right, I'm wrong.* It stung, but it was true. Even if the kid was a scammer, was lazy, and didn't want to work; and even if the girl with the skull-plastered shirt was an addict . . . I am wrong for having judged them. Had I chosen curiosity like Mollie, I could have at least acknowledged them with a wave, a smile, or some form of respect.

A week later, I was given another chance to do the right thing. Mollie and I were on our way home when I decided to make a quick stop for coffee and took a shortcut through the parking lot of a large shopping plaza. As I approached the exit, I noticed three bodies sitting on the grass—a young couple in their 20s along with an older-looking black Lab. In front of them were backpacks and camping supplies that propped up a sign saying, JUST NEED A LITTLE TRAVEL MONEY. ANYTHING HELPS.

The spot they'd claimed ensured drivers would not miss them. But despite their location only a few feet from the exit, most people chose not to stop. The four cars ahead of me even rolled through the stop sign and then quickly accelerated to beat the busy stream of traffic. Realizing that I'd be next to approach them, I began to fumble for my wallet, which was buried somewhere in my backpack. I dug frantically but couldn't find it. Other than a half-eaten bagel, I had nothing to give them. Now embarrassed and unsure what to do, I gently hit the gas pedal and started to drive away. At the *very second* that I did so, Mollie decided she had something to say. Looking at the couple and their canine companion to our right, she bellowed out a boisterous, *Woof!* I then looked over my shoulder and saw that the young woman was now smiling back at Mollie.

When I left the parking lot, the highway was directly in front of me. I thought to myself, *The easiest thing would be to jump on I-95 and head home. Besides, the idea of turning around feels too awkward. It would surely look strange if I suddenly returned after just passing by.* But if there's one thing I've learned from Mollie and this whole crazy process of loving everyone, it's that it takes courage.

Seeing me pull back in, the couple smiled and waved. Although their intent in choosing this spot was obvious, surprisingly, I saw no dollar signs in their eyes. Both had a look of contentment, and they acted genuinely happy to see me. Walking over, I said hello and slowly bent down to greet their dog. "Who's this pretty one?"

The young man, acting like a proud parent, said, "This is our girl, Katie."

Running my hand along her shiny coat, I replied, "She's beautiful."

"Yeah, man, she's my special girl." Leaning against the blonde to his left, he playfully nudged her with his elbow and assured, "You're *both* my special girls."

For several minutes, these two traveling soul mates shared their journey, telling me where they'd been and where they were hoping to go next. With a perfect blend of joy and tranquility, the woman said, "Sometimes people don't understand our lifestyle . . . but we just love being a part of the earth, connected to nature. We work on farms all over the country. It's not an easy life, but it's less stressful than doing something that doesn't make us happy."

Echoing her heartfelt statement, her partner spoke, "She's right, man. It's so freeing. Just being able to meet new people and travel is something everyone needs to try at least once. I don't look down on anybody's choices, but, man, it seems like living in a box would be really hard. To sleep in a box, drive one, work in one, get your entertainment from a box, and even communicate on a handheld box . . . that just doesn't seem like freedom. We were put here to expand, but if life is totally prepackaged, it sure can make it tough to find out who you really are." Looking down at Katie, he finished sharing his philosophies by saying, "Like her. She really gets it, man."

Something about his words really got to me. They had touched some nerve deep inside of my heart, and by the time he finished talking I had tears welling up in my eyes. He was so right—freedom is what we're all really looking for. We've been conditioned to think that the goal is happiness, but what we desire most is to be free from the emotional suffering that results from not living an authentic life. So many people become prisoners by believing that the boxes are the actual gifts! *We are the gift.*

After making a donation to help with their travel plans, I then offered a well-known gesture, which signifies the belief that within each of us there is a divine spark located in the center of the heart. Looking at all three, I placed my hands together in front of my chest, bowed my head, and said, "Namaste."

Folding their hands in prayer form, they returned the gesture, as both bowed back in my direction. This simple practice recognizes divinity in people first, looking beyond appearances, social standings, economics, politics, religion, race, sex, and age. *Namaste* traditionally means: I honor the place in you where the entire Universe resides. I honor the place of love, of light, of truth, of peace. I honor the place within you where if you are in that place in you and I am in that place in me, there is only one of us.

It's amazing how one word can say so much.

Chapter 13

Dealing with
Difficult Dogs

My peaceful morning walk was interrupted by an unusual amount of aggressive barking. An occasional yapper or two was nothing new to Mollie and me, but for whatever reason this day was packed with one mean-spirited mutt after another. It seemed that around every corner another canine was yelping in our direction or slamming its body up against a chain-link fence in an effort to reach us. These incidents were happening so often that I actually began to keep count. In the first 20 minutes there had been six incessant barkers, two fence slammers, and three vicious lunges from unfriendly dogs being walked by their owners. It all made for a rather interesting morning.

Toward the end of our walk I began to notice something quite extraordinary. We had just met up with a feisty Pomeranian who snarled at us from the end of his rope, which was secured to a small tree on the edge of the driveway. He pulled with such determination that it looked as if his eyes would pop out of his head. As we passed by, Mollie glanced over, flashed her signature smile . . . and kept moving. I was shocked. Normally she'd pull me over to at least get a quick sniff. But for some reason, she couldn't have cared less.

Each time a dog angrily barked our way or attempted to enter our space, she acted indifferent—even when a massive Saint Bernard charged at us from the other side of a wooden barricade. Built like Cujo, the rabid canine star of Stephen King's horror story, his powerful frame shook the wall (and me) so much that it nearly had me reaching for one of Mollie's poop bags! After this beast scared the bejesus out of me, I looked down to comfort Mollie. But evidently she didn't need it, as her tail was wagging and she seemed unaffected as she continued to happily prance down the street. Soon I began to wonder about what I would have done in a similar situation.

Had people been yelling at me as I took my morning stroll, I probably wouldn't have moved along so easily.

There is a wonderful story about the Buddha, which lines up with my interpretation of Mollie's composure that day:

> While walking through a city market one day, the Buddha was taunted by an old man sitting on a street corner. Glaring hatefully in the direction of the spiritual leader, the man began to yell, "You are nothing but a phony! There's nothing enlightened about you whatsoever—*you* should be bowing at *my* feet!" Continuing to curse vulgarities for all to hear, the old man screamed, "Go find another city to wander through! You are not welcome here!" This went on for several minutes as the Buddha simply smiled and continued walking.

> The next day, the Buddha returned to the marketplace, and once again the rabid old man was there, only this time his anger had intensified. He was cursing the Buddha's mother, father, and anyone who would follow his teachings. Crowds of people gathered and stared, many waiting to see if the Buddha would react with hostility, thus proving the old man's claims.

This went on for an entire week until finally one day, as the Buddha was leaving the market, the man approached him. Exhausted from his ranting, but also curious about the Buddha's secret to nonreaction, the man inquired, "Lord Buddha, I do not understand. Every day you arrive smiling, and each day I curse your name, but nothing moves you. You even reenter this city each day with joy, knowing all too well that I await you with my wicked tongue. How are you able to choose peace while I scream the worst things I can think of to your face?"

The Buddha, still beaming, looked at the old man and asked, "If a friend approached you offering a gift, but you declined to accept it, to whom does the gift belong?" Still weary from days of yelling, the man paused and thought carefully about his answer.

"Well, if I do not take it, then it still belongs to my friend."

The Buddha's eyes shone brightly as he said, "Ah yes, my friend, you are correct! So if I refuse your gifts of anger, hostility, and hatred, to whom do they belong?" Humbled, the man bowed, rose up, and began to walk the city streets praising the Buddha's name.

Many years ago, while on the basketball court during a pick-up game, a man taught me a valuable lesson about keeping my composure. I was a pretty decent ballplayer, but on that particular night I couldn't make a single shot against my opponent. I'd drive to the left, and he'd steal the ball from me. If I pulled up for a jumper, he'd swat it away into the hands of his teammate. Every time I touched the ball, things seemed to go horribly wrong. And here's where it got really interesting: not only was I playing against a man twice my age, but my antagonizing competitor only had one arm! The whole time on the court he pointed at his lost limb, calling himself "The One-Armed Bandit." Throughout the game he would yell out, "And the one-armed bandit *scoooores* again!" Or he'd look at me and say, "Can you believe a guy with one arm is kicking your ass?"

I couldn't.

I was flat-out furious, mostly with myself. This went on for quite a while, until I finally decided to let a friend sub for me. Physically I wasn't tired, but mentally I was completely spent. As I leaned against the wall beating myself up, trying to figure out what had happened to my once brilliant three-point shot, the One-Armed Bandit ran over to me, looked into my eyes, smiled, and said, "Hey, kid, if you want to win on the court and in life, don't let other people rent space in your head."

I snapped back, "What's that supposed to mean?" Tapping two fingers on his left temple, he spoke again, only this time, more slowly. "Up here . . . don't let others occupy this space. It's all yours. You own it . . . not other people."

I've never forgotten his words. The Bandit was the first person to teach me that *I* am the one in control of my thoughts, not anyone else. And the only way I can feel rejected, offended, or even treated poorly is by *allowing* other people to find and push my buttons. Still, this is a daily process, one I continue to work on 17 years after receiving the lesson. The spiritual path I've chosen has undeniably helped, but lately the space in my head has been fully occupied by the tenant from hell. And truth be told, the individual "renting" from me (my neighbor) almost ensured the book you are now holding would never be written. The thought of having to include her in my efforts to "love everyone" felt impossible.

Throughout my life, I've encountered some of the meanest SOBs you'd ever meet. Some have been family members, such as my paternal grandfather, a man who performed unspeakable acts of hatred and cruelty. Others have been malicious strangers, as in the man who kidnapped my sister when she was a teenager. Then there are those sadistic individuals on the evening news, often referred to as "society's worst." And on a much smaller scale, there are those who drive like mad, as if on suicide missions, nearly missing pedestrians such as Mollie and me. (On more than one occasion we've escaped being run down by a driver who was texting while behind the wheel.)

Somehow, through the grace of God and hours of meditation, I've found a place in my heart to forgive these people. Not condone; forgive. So as you can imagine, if I've let go of my anger toward those just mentioned, but not my neighbor who has recently been renting space in my head, she would have to be the most awful, vile, and unlovable being on the planet.

Not even close.

I wish I could explain it. I wish there was a logical answer. And I wish my bones didn't ache whenever I see her face. But they do. In my 42 years on this earth, I cannot recall a time when I've disliked someone more. I have many reasons for feeling this way, the least of which are that she is a stone-faced, cold-hearted, habitual liar; smokes too much weed;

contributes nothing to society; and takes as much as she possibly can from others. I'm also the first to recognize that these reasons do not justify my seething anger. Yes, I am the one with the problem.

Please don't misunderstand me—my neighbors often remark about her unfriendly demeanor and *very* strange ways, too. But unlike me, they refuse to give "Old Sourpuss" their precious time and energy. In fact, I'm the only one neurotically watching her every move, as I'm sent into a state of agitation at the sight of her car driving by. And with only a few buildings separating us, I'm given sufficient opportunities to make myself miserable.

Not only is this woman a royal pain in the you know what, she also has a *freakin' menace of a dog*. On multiple occasions, this four-legged nuisance has broken free from his leash, run into my yard, and viciously attacked Mollie. Thankfully, Mollie has never been seriously injured. But following each of these incidents, there hasn't once been an apology or the slightest hint of remorse from the dog's owner. She simply calls the hellhound back to her and gives him a cookie as they both hop onto her broom and fly away.

Recently, my feelings toward her have come full circle. Although I still pray that a U-Haul truck will pull into her driveway and take her far away, there's a much bigger battle that I've begun to fight—the one within myself. Perhaps what bothers me even more than my dislike toward her is the frustration I feel about my own negativity. As someone who is supposed to dedicate his life to kindness, peace, and unconditional love . . . lately there have been times when I've felt like a fraud.

I especially became aware of this inconsistency following the latest episode, when Mollie was attacked for the fourth time. I lost it. I almost could have justified my fury with the woman and her dog, but when I acted like a complete jerk toward my wife, friends, and anyone who dared approach me, that's when I decided that enough was enough. I was letting her win. She was "renting space in my head." My ill feelings toward her were poisoning my system and now infecting those I loved. This whole thing had haunted me long enough; it was time to get some help. So that afternoon, I contacted a friend.

John's perspective and Buddhist teachings had been so valuable throughout the summer, so I thought he might be able to shed some light on this current situation. It had been a few weeks since we'd seen each other, but once he received my message, he graciously offered to visit me at my home. Just knowing that he was coming to see me melted away the irritation that I'd been feeling all week.

After recapping the topics from a few of our earlier meetings, I then told him of my recent struggles and that I wasn't living congruently with my beliefs. I started by saying, "I've met some extremely difficult people over the years, most of whom I've been able to forgive and eventually release from my life, even at times wishing them peace. But over the past several months, I've been dealing with someone who's had me dangerously close to feeling something I promised myself that I'd never feel: hatred."

John began with one question. "Is this a person you see every day?"

"No. Not every single day, but often enough. She lives in my neighborhood."

Sitting tall as if in meditation, John folded his hands in front of him and listened while I vented. "She's done some very unkind things since moving here, but I won't go into all of the details. My issue with this woman right now is her vicious dog." John remained fully engaged while I explained how Mollie had been attacked on several occasions without a single apology from the owner. Finally, I finished with, "I've tried many different practices to remove this hatred that I feel toward her from my heart, but nothing is working. I was hoping you might be able to offer me something that would help me let go of these negative feelings."

John's response was the last thing I expected to hear. Laughing wholeheartedly, he said, "I know these things all too well—I'm full of anger myself!" Hearing this immediately put me at ease. He continued, "So here's the deal: what helps me is just understanding . . . and applying the understanding. This can be difficult. First of all, we must ask ourselves, 'Does this woman have anyone who loves her—a husband, a family member, or a friend? Does *anyone* like this person?'"

My ego immediately jumped in. "Maybe her husband does, but nobody else in the neighborhood likes her!"

Smiling, John asked, "Does the dog like her? She feeds him, right?"

"Yes."

"So then he probably likes her . . . would you say that's correct?"

I didn't want to admit it, but I finally said, "Yes, I suppose the dog likes her."

John then went more deeply into this philosophy. "What we want to understand here is that she isn't inherently bad. If the dog and her husband do not see her as you do, then she isn't innately a horrible person. That being said, this woman is just karma; she's a reflection of something in your past, and these things come up all the time. It's no coincidence that you're writing a book about Mollie and there's a dog attacking her and, in a sense, you. It's all karma, brother. Even the Buddha said that one of the hardest things we have to figure out is our karma. It's such a tough thing. *Especially* when dealing with someone who lives so close! More anger erupts from neighborhood feuds than any other place. The mind is constantly marking its territory, and when a person or even a pet comes onto our property, we want to attack!"

John's words hit home. He was right. I felt like they were trespassing, even acting like criminals, each time she and the dog came onto my property. He continued, "First, let's understand that these issues of personal property create even more anger. Next, we need to realize that she isn't inherently bad; only her actions are. Finally, we need to find a resolution. And the most logical thing you can do to eliminate old karma is practice the opposite of what she does to upset you the most."

Now I was confused. "I'm not sure I know what you mean."

"What I'm asking you to do, Michael, is act in ways that she does not. For example, this woman allows her dog to attack. If you're presented with any situation where you know Mollie could be aggressive toward another dog, make the kinder choice by pulling her back before a problem could arise. Another example is her cold attitude toward people. The opposite, of course, is to be friendly and warm when you meet others. If she takes from others all the time, then you need to give! In doing the opposite, you're releasing your old karma, which is somehow allowing her negative presence in your life."

Slowly, I was starting to get it—her actions and presence both related to unkind things I had once done. She was a mirror to the choices I'd made from my current life or, as Buddhism often teaches, a past one. This stung, because it was making me responsible. In other words, her being a part of my life . . . was my fault. But by choosing to do what's right, I could ultimately make this woman (my bad karma) disappear.

John then placed his hands to his chest and said, "The only way this will work is if you do it with a loving heart." Seeing my apprehension, he told me, "Don't worry. It's not necessary to direct your love and kindness toward her; perhaps one day you can if you're ready, but right now you only need to practice what she does not. And it's important to remember that you have to do so with the intention of getting rid of this angry, karmic energy that you're carrying around. So dedicate any kindnesses that you do to releasing her from your life. Soon, you'll begin to see this woman less and less . . . and even create the likelihood that she'll move away. Guaranteed."

"Honestly, that's exactly what I wish for every time she drives by. Just seeing her car makes me mad! Or if I hear her dog bark, I immediately feel agitated."

John laughed and asked, "How is that even possible? Like her, the car doesn't have an inherent nature of badness. If it did, I'd get upset when I saw it, too! The same goes for the dog's bark—it's just a sound, only decibels, right? Your own perception of it is what makes you anxious."

John wasn't done. He wanted me to grasp the other things that were happening, or rather not happening. "Tell me, what does this woman act like when she sees you? Does she say anything abusive?"

"Not so much with words; it's mostly her face. She always has a look of irritation and gives everyone the evil eye."

"So you're saying that it's not just at *you*, right?"

"Well . . . I guess when I think about it, she looks at everybody that way."

"Exactly. So it's not personal. But beyond that, here's where we need to look at our level of understanding again, realizing the truth about this woman: *she's suffering tremendously.* This doesn't justify her actions, but it does tell us that she's in emotional pain. So try to judge less and understand more. The more you can understand people, the more you can love them."

This made total sense. Anyone who looks and acts the way she does would have to be miserable. I was almost embarrassed when I acknowledged this, since it's the very thing I teach at my seminars, that the primary cause of unkindness is unhappiness. At my talks I also discuss the importance of having compassion for those who are suffering. Evidently, I needed a reminder of these lessons if I was going to continue teaching them.

I then said to John, "Lately, what bothers me more than her and the dog is the fact that I've allowed this hatred into my heart. It goes against everything I believe."

He replied with, "Hey, look, we're human, right? These things happen."

"But I don't want hatred in my heart; it's just not right."

"It's not hatred; don't overdramatize. It's only heavy anger that you're experiencing." It was true. I'd turned this whole issue into my own little drama party, and the longer we talked, the more I began to realize how ridiculous the situation was. Yes, I had to protect Mollie. But as far as this woman went, I had to let go and move on.

As we wrapped up our conversation, John made my assignment clear: "So again, I want you to practice the *opposite* of whatever she does to you; turn it around by performing a positive act toward someone else. And it must be done with pure intent and love. This is the quickest way to dissolve your old karma. Take it a step farther, though. Each night before bed, write down at least three things you did during that day that were dedicated to setting yourself free. It might be too much right now, but at some point maybe you could even do a random act of kindness for her. And finally, continue to understand that neither she nor her dog is bad. Their actions may be, but, again, this is not inherently who they are. By understanding this, you create a little more space in your heart. Capiche?"

Less than an hour had passed since John arrived, but I already felt a shift taking place. My mind was clear, and my heart had even begun to unclench. He suggested that we meet at the end of the week to check on my progress. Before leaving, he gave me one final piece of advice. "I know you're very upset by all of this, but try to be lighter about it. It's really not a big deal." I nodded in agreement. It was true; I definitely needed to lighten up.

No surprise, the very next day I was put to the test. While out for a walk, Mollie and I passed my neighbor's house while she was outside attempting to move a large appliance. When she saw me, she stuck her nose in the air, shunning me. But I felt no anger as I recalled John's words: "She's suffering tremendously." Upon seeing her and her frail husband wrestle with the refrigerator they were moving, I decided to send kind thoughts their way. This wasn't easy, but it was a small victory.

Later that evening, a friend of mine who lives next to the woman sent me a text. He's no fan of hers either, but has occasionally offered to help her out. Just recently he told me how she'd suckered him into moving some large items from her garage. So when his text said, *I need you to help me with something tonight,* I jokingly replied, *Help you move stuff for sourpuss?* He knows how I feel about her and that I have no desire to help this woman, which is why his reply nearly made me throw up: *Yes.*

This was no coincidence. The Universe's twisted sense of humor was clearly testing my willingness to practice loving everyone, while also giving me an opportunity to eradicate a ton of bad karma. Even my friend's text was clearly a part of some crazy cosmic plan. So, taking in the deepest breath I perhaps have ever taken, I typed back: *Okay, see you in five minutes.*

He responded: *Meet me at my place first.*

When I got to his driveway, surprisingly I felt very little apprehension. Had this request happened before my conversation with John, I'm sure I would have reacted differently. But because of my wise friend's guidance, I felt that no matter how poorly this woman treated me, I was going to be okay. As I stood outside, I didn't see my neighbor anywhere, so I decided to call him. When he answered his phone, I said, "Are you ready?"

He replied, "Come inside."

Walking up his steps, I still didn't feel stressed. I even did a positive visualization, seeing the whole thing as being peaceful and drama free. When I made my way through the kitchen, my friend immediately yelled at me, "You have to do something about this woman. Get rid of her—she's driving me nuts!"

I wasn't expecting this. "What happened? What do you mean?" I asked.

Pointing to his computer, he spoke with fervor again: "I need you to block this person's e-mails; how do you do it?" Then I recalled a recent conversation about how he was being bombarded with photos and e-garbage from an acquaintance of his.

Since he knows I work on a computer all day, he figured that I could make this annoyance disappear. "Okay, that's no problem. I can block her." But I had something much bigger on my mind: "So are we going next door to move stuff first?"

He looked at me, laughed, and then replied, "I was messing with you about that. I only needed help with my e-mail."

Two days later I met with John for coffee. When I sat across from him, he grinned and immediately asked, "So, how are things going? Have you been working on the ideas we discussed?" I went on to tell him about my friend's text and my response.

He said, "Just the intent alone cleansed you of much karma. Your willingness to do this act was a huge step forward. And remember, tackling the *really* ugly stuff in our lives with a good heart is what moves us closer to enlightenment."

Looking at John, I asked him the question I'd been meaning to ask him all summer: "When people become enlightened, will they automatically love everyone, or do they have to love everyone first?"

Without hesitation he replied, "It works both ways, brother."

PART III

A New Leash on Life

Chapter 14

24 Hours of Kindness

After hugging Mollie tight, I told her I loved her and would be back soon. She knew I'd be gone for a few days as she eyed my bags by the door, and the look on her face nearly broke my heart. Her expression was a blend of confusion and sadness. Leaving her created more anxiety in me than I'd anticipated, but I knew this trip was important. Ultimately, it would be the ideal opportunity to practice the things I'd learned from her over the summer, while also taking John's advice to rebuild my good karma.

I'd been asked to travel to New Jersey to lead a group of people during an event called 24 Hours of Kindness. I'd created this annual marathon of goodwill in 2008, putting The Kindness Center on the map, and it continues to grow in popularity each year. When I posted the following announcement on my Facebook page, it inspired people around the world to join us:

> *On July 27th, The Kindness Center and the Joseph Lapinski Foundation are joining forces for The Kindness Center's most celebrated event: 24 Hours of Kindness. From 9 in the morning on Friday until 9 in the morning on Saturday, we will be on the streets of New Jersey and New York City for a nonstop marathon of performing acts of kindness. Our goal is to inspire, uplift, and change as many lives as possible during this 24-hour period. We hope that wherever you are on Friday and Saturday, you will join us, taking the time to brighten someone's life in your own unique way. Together, we can change the world . . . one small act of kindness at a time!*
>
> *Peace & Love,*
> *Michael*

Once I arrived at the airport, I started to get excited. I'm one of those strange people who actually enjoy the insanity of traveling by air. Each time I fly, I know I'll meet someone interesting or come home with a new story to tell. And I was confident that this day would be no different. I've also found a se-cret defense tool when it comes to battling the un-kindness that can accompany flying: *a T-shirt.* This is not just any T-shirt, mind you; this one has magical powers. It's solid black with just four words written in white across the front, and whenever people catch a glimpse of it, they either smile or say, "Amen!" It says: Be Good to People. This simple statement is now a global movement created by my good friend Kris-sy, who is the founder of Be Good to People.

When I made my way to security, my expecta-tions and positive affirmations were met—no one was in line. I walked up, handed over my passport, and was soon throwing my bags up on the conveyor belt for x-rays. Once I was waved through the metal detector, a guard smiled and said, "I love your shirt!"

Her comment prompted a woman to stare in my direction and reiterate the sentiment: "I love it!"

I still had over an hour before my flight depart-ed, so I made a quick stop for a bottle of water. I was relaxed and happy, and my guilt over leaving Mollie had subsided. My original thought was that her lessons in loving everyone would come in handy during the 24 Hours of Kindness, but evidently the Universe had other plans. Just as I was walking into my terminal, the woman at the desk grabbed the microphone and relayed the message no one wanted to hear: "Your flight has been delayed. We are now looking at a 3 P.M. departure for the 11 A.M. flight to Newark, New Jersey."

I took in a deep breath and sat down. I had a few books to occupy me and decided that the delay wasn't going to ruin my good mood. At the same time, other flights had also been rescheduled due to bad weather. Evidently, the passengers from these flights hadn't brought anything to read, since they were soon rushing to the counter, firing off one angry comment after another. It wasn't long before the airline employee kindly told everyone to be seated and that she would call travelers up one at a time. One by one, they approached to tell her what she should or should not do. They acted like school-yard bullies. Watching this was actually disturbing and a reminder that there's still a huge deficiency in kindness in the world. Finally, I stood up, got in line, and was about to dedicate my next act to my sister, Lisa, who works at Delta Airlines. She'd told me stories of people behaving this way, but to witness it was altogether different.

When it was my turn, the woman at the counter could barely look up. She'd taken such a beating from the other passengers that she was now cowering. Still looking down, she timidly asked, "May I help you?"

I paused and waited until she looked up to reply. "Hi. I just want to make a comment, because it's probably not something you hear often enough. First of all, my sister works for an airline, so I *know* how difficult this job can be." Her face softened. I then continued speaking, only louder so the other passengers could hear me. "From where I've been sitting, it's obvious that you have one of the toughest jobs in the world. And I just want you to know how much I appreciate your friendly attitude and all that you're doing to accommodate us. You're doing an awesome job."

Her eyes moistened. She looked bashfully at me and replied, "You're right. It's not often someone says that. Thank you—that means so much to me."

When I turned around to return to my seat, the roles had been reversed; the woman behind the counter was smiling, and the hotheaded passengers were now gazing at the floor. Those who did look up got an eyeful; the first thing they saw was BE GOOD TO PEOPLE on the front of my chest. One lady walked right up to me and exclaimed, "That's an awesome T-shirt!" The energy in the terminal had shifted. And although I take no credit for this miracle, 20 minutes later the 3:00 departure time was changed to 12:30.

Once my flight landed, I met my friend Bill and his wife Karen outside the airport. They are two of the most genuine, good-hearted people you could ever meet. For Bill, this 24 Hours of Kindness held a special meaning. Several years ago, he started the Joseph Lapinski Foundation in honor of his grandfather, who passed away from cancer. Affectionately known as "Pop," he was remembered for his kind deeds, and this event was a way to honor his legacy. I soon learned that there would be a thoughtfully assembled crew of nine volunteers, including myself, along with an itinerary that would keep us going for the entire 24 hours.

That evening I was invited to have dinner with Bill's nana, who was Pop's wife. Bill thought it would be nice for me to meet her and a few other family members before our big day. From the moment I walked through Nana's door, it felt like I was home. Her warm embrace and contagious smile immediately made me wish she were my nana! At 88 years old, she's an inspiration to all who know her . . . and even to those she'll never meet. Because of her, our kindness crew had over 50 handcrafted quilts to deliver the next morning.

Following dinner, we began to assemble backpacks, which would be given to children at local hospitals. Each would contain a homemade quilt, toys, books, stickers, and other goodies. Then we opened the box UPS had delivered just an hour before. Enclosed were uniforms for our 24-hour mission. Bill had ordered T-shirts for everyone participating, which read, POWERED BY KINDNESS.

Back at my hotel room, getting six hours of sleep was the best I could do, which was not bad considering how excited I was when my head hit the pillow. Before I knew it, Bill was pulling up in front of the hotel to pick everyone up at 8:30 A.M. To have a group of people with so much heart almost guaranteed that the event was going to be a huge success. Each member of our crew was unique in his or her own way, but we all shared a vision of creating a kinder world. The van was loaded down with the backpacks, flowers to randomly hand out, poster board for making FREE HUGS signs, and even a few hundred pounds of freshly picked corn. An organization called America's Grow a Row had donated it to our event, giving us the opportunity to deliver the corn to a local soup kitchen.

Our first destination was the Emmanuel Cancer Foundation to drop off Friday-night-fun kits for the kids. Each bag held DVDs, a quilt, popcorn, and other items for enjoying a Friday evening. Walking into the cramped office space, it was obvious that they ran the program on a shoestring budget. Shelves of food, school supplies, and other donated items were in the open, making it clear that the office doubled as a supply closet. Despite a lack of funding, the group was making a huge difference. Their mission statement read:

> *The Emmanuel Cancer Foundation is committed to being a beacon of light for New Jersey families of children diagnosed with cancer. Through trained professionals and dedicated volunteers, our goal is to replace fear with hope and confusion with balance.*

But perhaps even more touching than this declaration were the crayon masterpieces and photos of smiling children that covered the walls. These images told the bigger story.

We were soon on the road again, driving to our next stop, Valley Hospital. Here we would donate a large pile of quilts to The Butterflies Program. They provide full-care services that offer comfort and relief to infants and young ones who have been diagnosed with life-limiting or life-threatening illnesses. Special care is also available in homes, where children can be most comfortable. The program gives support for the children's parents, siblings, and extended family members, too.

Bill had scheduled the drop-off and our meeting with the program director for 11 A.M., but we had arrived early. Rather than remain idle for the next 45 minutes, we ventured into the hospital café in hopes of buying coffee for unsuspecting customers. When we walked in, there didn't appear to be a lot of activity, as only two tables were occupied. Seeing our POWERED BY KINDNESS T-shirts and our arms full of quilts, the waitress looked at us with curiosity. We told her who we were and the reason for our visit. She became excited and praised our plans for the day, and then asked about the handmade quilts. No surprise, she knew Nana!

Bill told the waitress to give him the tab for the customers who were in the café. This would be our first spontaneous act of the morning. His gesture sparked excitement and gratitude, and it also guided us to the perfect person as we were beginning our day. Seated at one of the tables was a hospital volunteer named Paul, who still seemed full of vitality at 82. I noticed that, like Nana, his eyes were clear and filled with glowing light. From the moment he spoke, we all knew that we'd be leaving inspired and perhaps a little wiser.

Paul talked about his secrets to 56 years of marriage, the technological changes he'd witnessed over the years, his relationship with God, and the vast importance of good health. But most of all, he wanted to talk about love. He made it clear that expressing love and helping people were the main reasons we should get out of bed each day, not money or material possessions. He also put emphasis on letting others know how much you care about them, because, "There are no guarantees for tomorrow." Paul knew this firsthand. With tears in his eyes, he shared how he'd experienced the devastating loss of two children, saying, "Hug your kids, and tell them you love them every chance you get."

Several heartwarming stories later, he was still going: "Okay, I just want to tell you this *one* last story, and then I'll let you kids go!" We all laughed, since it was the third time he'd made this declaration. He laughed, too, but promised, "This is really the last one!" His coffee-sipping partner looked up at me and winked as if to say, *Young man, you could be stuck right here for your entire 24 hours.* The truth is that if we had, I'm not sure any of us would have minded.

We gathered around like disciples as Paul began his final tale. "One summer when I was a little boy,

I went camping with my family. We were all staying in cabins that sat on a beautiful lake. I remember one evening just before dusk when my father asked for my help. He simply needed me to deliver a lantern to another cabin a short ways from where we were staying. I was so excited! To be given this task and allowed to go off on my own made me feel like such a big kid. Once my dad filled the lantern with kerosene and showed me the path to take, I was off!

"When I was about halfway there, something terrible happened. I can't recall what I tripped on, but all of a sudden I found myself sailing through the air . . . and then heard the sound of the lantern smashing into a hundred pieces. I was devastated, crying, and very scared. Picking up the shards of glass, I thought, *What will the man in the cabin do for light, and what if he yells at me?*

"Walking up the steps to his door, I felt sick to my stomach. I was almost too terrified to knock, but I did. And when the old man opened the door, he immediately noticed the broken lantern in my hands. He also knew I'd been crying. I started to tell him how sorry I was, but he stopped me. The old man bent down, smiled warmly, and said, 'It's okay, son. I know you tried your very best . . . and that's all that matters.'"

As Paul finished his story, he began to cry. He wiped tears from his eyes and tried to apologize, but we would hear none of it. His sensitivity and gentleness touched our hearts deeply. He then echoed his feelings: "Ever since that day, I've never forgotten the old man's lesson, knowing that as long as I try my best, everything will be okay."

His story was exactly what each of us needed to hear. Understandably, a few members of our kindness crew (including me) had been anticipating the outcome of this event before it had even begun. To have lofty expectations for a day of this significance was perfectly normal. After all, we were out to *change the world!* But Paul's wisdom was a sweet reminder that all we really needed to do was our best. It was about quality, not quantity. Whether we touched one life or hundreds, what mattered most was that our hearts were fully engaged in each moment. And the next 22 hours would offer us endless opportunities to focus on just that.

By the time we left the hospital, our emotions were running high, and everyone in the van was buzzing. With each stop we made, the momentum and positive energy increased. This was the third time in four years that I'd done this event, but for the others it was a new experience altogether. To see their enthusiasm gave me a feeling of gratitude. I was honored to be among them. I missed Cara and Mollie very much, but it felt good to have a change of pace for a few days. I'd been writing about love and enlightenment for months, and it was time to put everything I had learned to the test.

We were now en route to Eva's Village, a soup kitchen located in Paterson, New Jersey. Our mission was to simply drop off the huge bags of corn that were donated and then take a tour of the facilities. Most of us had worked in soup kitchens before, so we figured this visit would be brief. Other than a kitchen, dining area, and stockroom, there typically isn't a lot to see. Little did we know that Eva's Village was no ordinary place; it actually *is* a village.

As we pulled into the parking lot just before lunchtime, we saw hundreds of men, women, and children waiting in line for a meal. I had witnessed this in my own town, but on a much smaller scale. Scenes like this bother me tremendously, because I know the anxiety that comes from not being able to buy food. Fortunately, I've never had to wait in such a line. Unfortunately, though, there were hundreds, maybe thousands, of people in this town who would never be able to say the same.

Once inside, we met with several upbeat staff members. They called our attention to a detailed map of Eva's Village. It was incredible. What had started as a tiny kitchen 30 years ago had evolved into so much more. As the vision of how to help the poor expanded, facilities were added and now this organization occupies a well-maintained campus of 12 buildings that cover three blocks in downtown Paterson. There's no other place quite like it in the country. Their mission is to feed the hungry, shelter the homeless, treat the addicted, and provide free medical and dental care to the poor. They also offer no-cost child care, yoga and meditation classes, spiritual guidance, and a wide array of other compassionate services. And they do it all with respect and dignity for each individual.

During the tour, each of us continued looking around with wide eyes and changed hearts. We were mostly in awe of the guests. Whether it was in the dining area or the drug-and-alcohol treatment center, each time we met new people, they always greeted us with warmth and respect. Perhaps one of the most inspiring moments was visiting the dental clinic. The walls were covered with before-and-after photos of men and women who had received extensive dental work. This free service was provided not only to restore smiles, but also to boost the individuals' spirits, giving them the confidence needed to reenter the workforce.

When it was time to leave, we hugged the staff, thanking them for their hospitality, and vowed to return one day soon. Driving away, there was a brief moment of silence throughout the van. Eva's Village had affected each of us in a deep way. I'd spent my summer reflecting on the path of unconditional love, but never in my wildest dreams did I expect to find its truest meaning in New Jersey. And while passing burned-out buildings, piles of trash, and despondent-looking souls on the streets, it hit me. I realized that the staff at Eva's, and my guru Mollie, share the same philosophy: they *love and accept everyone,* even those under the direst conditions. This includes drug addicts; the homeless; the unemployed; and those who are unshaven, toothless, drunken, incoherent, and swearing like parrots—*everyone.*

On many occasions during our morning walks, Mollie and I have encountered individuals with these very traits. Each time we do, her reaction is always the same—joy, enthusiasm, and the desire to know the person better. She adheres to the suggestion often made by great spiritual teachers: See everyone you meet as God in disguise.

Everyone agreed that it would be a good idea to grab a slice of pizza before our next stop. Bill generously paid for everybody's lunch, so I decided to pass it on by paying for a customer who was already ordering. At first he seemed confused, looking around and joking, "Where's the hidden camera?" But after noticing my T-shirt, he gratefully accepted and left wearing a huge smile.

Saint Barnabas Medical Center was next. Here we dropped off 30 backpacks for the Family Reach Foundation. This is another wonderful place that's dedicated to providing compassionate care and financial relief for children and families who are fighting cancer. As we'd noticed with the other programs we'd given to earlier in the day, the people involved were extraordinary. They were so much more than volunteers or staffers; they were changing the world one life at a time. In addition to the backpacks, Bill also made a donation from The Joseph Lapinski Foundation—$20,000!

Because of my experience with random acts of kindness, the group was now looking to me for leadership, as a more spontaneous phase of our journey was about to begin. When we got to our next stop, Bill said, "Okay, Michael, this is where you can show us how it's done!" Being far from home and not familiar with my surroundings, I was a little nervous. Many of the people we would encounter don't speak English, but then I remembered what I have so often told others: *Kindness is a universal language, which anyone can speak.* All races, religions, genders, and ages understand the power of the human heart.

We decided to start simply. Bill's Aunt Dottie, who owns a floral shop, had donated several bouquets of carnations. Flowers, like a smile, are a world-wide symbol of love and happiness, and are always the perfect way to brighten someone's day. Each of us grabbed a couple dozen carnations and ventured down the street in search of people who needed a gesture of kindness. At first, we handed them out to a few women and children as they were leaving local shops. But as we were doing this, I noticed a group of older kids rambunctiously darting down the sidewalk, which gave me an idea.

Stopping them, I said, "Hey, guys, how'd you like to help us do random acts of kindness?" Their faces went blank. I continued, "Would you be willing to take these flowers and just randomly give them away to people?"

This caught their interest, as each responded with a categorical, "Oh yeah!"

I then put emphasis on the fact that these were *free* flowers. Half joking with the tallest kid, I said, "Remember, don't try to sell them!" Upon agreeing with this condition, he and the others each took a fistful of pink carnations and were off and running.

After handing out the rest of the flowers, we decided to make a poster that read: FREE COFFEE . . . IF YOU TELL ME A HEARTWARMING STORY. Standing in front of Dunkin' Donuts, it took only minutes before a vibrant young woman approached me, wanting to share her tale of kindness. Halfway through her story, she began to cry, explaining how she'd just fed a mother and little boy who were living on the streets. She told me that she had two young children, and the sight of the homeless mother and son broke her heart. Speaking in a thick accent, she said with compassion, "I do not understand . . . how can the richest country in the world allow its people to go hungry? It does not seem right." I couldn't have agreed more.

It was getting close to sunset as we headed to New York City. Our first act of kindness in The Big Apple was buying ice cream for a family in Times Square. Stepping in line behind them, I said, "Hold on, my friends. This one's on me!" The mother looked at me as if I had popsicles coming out of my ears. "I'm serious. I'd love to pay," I told her. I motioned to my gang standing ten feet away, all displaying POWERED BY KINDNESS across their chests. "My friends and I are doing random acts of kindness, and you've been tagged. Just pass it on to another person someday, okay?"

They all smiled widely and thanked me. The ice-cream man winked at me and said, "That's pretty cool stuff you just did there, man!"

While we were trying to decide on our next move, a young man approached us wanting to know who we were and what we were doing. This bright, idealistic 19-year-old had traveled from the South two months before to pursue his dream of becoming a professional musician. He radiated optimism. He also told us how we could be of service to people in the area. "It's really hot out here, and one of the things the homeless really need is water. If you could buy a case and hand bottles out to them, they'd definitely appreciate it." As he continued talking about those living on the streets, it was obvious that he had tremendous compassion. We soon found out why he understood these people's needs so well. He was living in a shelter several blocks away.

As we continued walking through the city, we came across a man we nicknamed The Philosopher.

He offered us his wisdom in riddlelike form in exchange for bus fare: "If you were an instrument on the dashboard of a car, which one would you be?"

Confused, we replied, "Huh?"

He asked again. "Come on, think about it for a moment. Picture all the instruments that make your car work and ask yourself, *Which one am I?*"

The Philosopher then waited until each of us gave him our answers. "The engine," some said.

"Lights," was another reply.

"The steering wheel," said another.

Because my mind was going back and forth, I blurted out, "Windshield wipers!"

"Nah, you got it all wrong. Each day you choose which way you're going. Each day you decide. Each day you are the one who goes left or right. If you were an instrument on a car, you'd be the directional. The road you take in this life is up to you."

I pondered his words as we continued down the street. The lights and visual displays surrounding us had me staring up in wonder. I was especially in awe of the gigantic advertisements for *The Dark Knight Rises,* a movie I'd waited four years to see. On one corner, a huge poster for this latest Batman flick literally covered an entire building.

The film's release had been tainted by a horrific incident that happened exactly one week before in

Aurora, Colorado. During a midnight showing of the movie, a lone gunman dressed in tactical clothing walked into the audience and fired multiple rounds of bullets, killing 12 people and injuring 58 others. The news of this tragedy and the stories that followed were devastating.

While standing there gazing at the massive billboard, I felt a positive shift, which gave me an idea—one that would eventually become an unforgettable part of our night. I asked one of my friends to check her iPhone for some information. We discovered that the *Aquilegia coerulea* (also known as the Colorado blue columbine) is the state flower of Colorado. Since it was late at night, the nearest street vendor we found had a limited selection, but he did have a supply of one blue species that we all felt would be perfect. The midnight showing of *The Dark Night Rises* would be ending soon, so we quickly made our way to the theater, divided the flowers among us, and eagerly waited for the patrons to come down the escalator and into the lobby.

When the first wave of people began to descend, my heart started pounding. It was hard to say how they'd react. A part of me even worried that they might think we were a religious group or a cult. But as each individual glided down the escalator, noticing our matching shirts and blue flowers in our extended hands, rather than a look of apprehension, there was reverence in their eyes. In silence, men, women, and teens alike accepted our gestures without asking why. They knew. No words were needed, as each flower was received with honor and gratitude. Most people looked directly into our eyes, and many even bowed their heads. As Bill would note later that evening, "Coming down the escalator, they looked at peace, even relieved, that they left the theater without incident." Bill was right—especially since there had been scares in other movie theaters that week. For this audience, seeing us at the door was perhaps a quiet way to celebrate their safe departure and a reminder to pray for those who had been affected in Colorado.

The vibe on the streets had noticeably changed. New York City is an intense place to begin with, but at three in the morning, it can definitely put you on edge. These were the hours when Manhattanites were either sleeping or staggering down the sidewalks. We never felt in danger, but still decided it was best to stick close together. Walking past a park, we saw that it had been closed off in a way that discouraged anyone from entering during the night. We contemplated heading back to our cars, but while talking about our next move, Bill heard a noise coming from the stairs that led down to the subway.

Hunched over and walking backward up the concrete steps was an older gentleman struggling with a cart that held all of his belongings. Bill was the first to react. He gently spoke to the man, "Hey, can I give you a hand with that?"

I then joined Bill as we each grabbed an end of the metal carriage and pulled it up to the street. With sincere gratitude, the man thanked us. Originally, I thought he was hunched over because of his position on the stairs, but I was wrong. Sadly, his curved spine was a permanent condition.

Now in his mid-60s, Randy had been homeless for quite some time. We were unsure what had caused his bent posture, but we did learn that the sores on his legs and feet were diabetes related. His health had deteriorated while living on the street, but overall he seemed happy. He said that he left the place where he was living because, "The stuff they were doing just ain't right." As a recovering addict, he felt that living "out here" was a better option than being around drugs and alcohol.

Slowly twisting his head up, Randy looked at

Bill and said, "When I heard your voice call out to help me, I knew God sent me a good person." This seemed to touch Bill's heart deeply.

Soon everyone moved in closer, wanting to know more about this kind man who rolled the contents of his entire life behind him in a three-by-four-foot cart. I put my arm on his shoulder and said, "What can we do for you tonight? We want to help you in any way we can."

Looking up at me, he gazed deep into my eyes. It was brief, but our connection made me feel as if I was in the presence of pure grace. With tenderness in his voice, he replied, "Well, I didn't eat dinner last night . . . some food would be real nice. A fish sandwich from McDonald's would be great. Just fish and cheese though, *no* sauce, okay?" He then had one last request: "There's a little store next to McDonald's. Would it be okay to have a bottle of water and . . . a TWIX bar? You know, the kind that has caramel in the middle." It was such a sweet, simple request from a man who had so little.

I asked Randy to wait while I went to get his meal. As I began walking away, I looked back and witnessed a beautiful scene. Now having guests in his "home," Randy took newspaper pages out of his cart, gently placed them on the steps, and then asked everyone to sit down.

When I got back, Randy was still playing the role of gracious host. The expressions on the faces of those around him made it apparent that he'd shared many nuggets of wisdom while I was gone. I walked over to his cart, which had a cardboard lid on top of it, and placed his meal down. Slowly rising, he smiled with delight and said, "Thank you so much! Wonderful, just wonderful." I then dumped out the contents of the second bag: several large TWIX bars. Laughing with joy, he clapped his hands as if I had just performed a magic trick. "Wowww . . . look at 'em all!"

Joking, I playfully reprimanded him by saying, "Don't you dare eat all of these tonight!"

When it was time to say good-bye, he pulled me close, and we simultaneously whispered the same words into each other's ear: "God bless you, my friend." This experience was an eye-opener for me, a reminder that although much can be done in 24 hours, kindness has to be 365 days a year if we're really going to change the world.

By 4:00 A.M., we were out of the city and making our way back to Paterson. Although it hadn't felt totally safe in the daytime, pulling back into town at

this hour made us feel quite apprehensive. Visually, it reminded me of a Tim Burton movie. The humid weather and cloudy skies combined with a burning building nearby gave the skyline a dramatic, eerie feeling. Thankfully, it would be light soon.

Still, we needed to find a way to keep busy until the streets became fully alive again. Recognizing a familiar pink-and-orange neon sign in the distance, we decided to begin there. Like us, the all-night Dunkin' Donuts was open 24 hours, ready to serve.

While I was buying breakfast for a group of city workers, Bill was also at the counter purchasing two orders of Box O' Joe (a cardboard container that holds 8 cups of coffee) and two dozen donuts that we planned to give to the homeless. As we were about to leave, a man who had been sitting alone with his laptop approached us, curious about our mission. His name was Alberto. He'd been a resident of Paterson, but not a happy one, for over 30 years. The frustration in his voice was only overshadowed by the sadness in his eyes.

For the next 20 minutes he told us stories of crime, corruption, and the decay of what had once been a great city. He then discussed the homeless population, which was now close to 1,000, showing us photos that he'd taken of families living on the riverbanks. Finally, he talked about the drug problems and gang population. Hearing these accounts suddenly made me feel grateful for where I live. As we left, Alberto informed us about a park just down the road that would surely have people sleeping on its benches.

Light was just starting to break as we drove through the center of town, and small signs of life began to appear. Lit cigarettes in darkened doorways and a scattering of pedestrians were clues that the city was waking up.

When we arrived at the park, there were many people asleep outside. I slowly walked up to a man I noticed lying on the ground. Seeing the box of coffee in my hands, he rose up, rubbed his eyes, and immediately accepted my offer. "Sweet and light," were his first words.

Just to be sure, I asked, "Do you mean sugar and a little cream?"

"Sweet and light," he repeated. After I'd poured him a cup, he barked loudly toward the gazebo: "TJ, wake up, man!"

I looked in the direction he was yelling and saw a man, woman, and teenage boy covered in blankets. Nobody moved. He called out again, "TJ! Wake up!" This time the man who was sitting in a broken office chair moved his head. Although there was no sun, he wore dark sunglasses to cover his eyes. The older man pointed at the box of coffee, which seemed to do the trick.

I walked up to the gazebo and began to talk with the family, who were all extremely polite and grateful for our gifts. TJ's larger-than-life personality especially had me hooked. Although I couldn't see his eyes, both his massive smile and huge arms were features that were hard to overlook. Joking, I said, "Man, what's a guy gotta do to get pipes like that?"

Smiling wider, TJ replied, "Donuts, man, lots and lots of donuts."

I laughed and came back with, "You don't build muscle like that from sugar and flour."

"Nah, I'm just messin' with ya. I actually practice many styles of martial arts." Now I was excited! As a onetime wannabe kung fu master, I couldn't wait to hear what he had to say. Growing up, I was obsessed with Bruce Lee, Chuck Norris, Jackie Chan, and anyone who could leap through the air and land the perfect spinning back kick.

But TJ surprised me. Rather than relaying stories about destroying an opponent with a five-finger death punch, he talked about harmony, peacefulness, and connecting with the elements of the earth.

"Physical strength is an illusion," he said. "The same goes for weapons. The mind is the only tool that really matters. It can create war or brotherhood. Peace is the way of the true martial artist. Yeah, man . . . always choose the path of peace." His words made the comments of The Philosopher from the night before seem even more relevant. The power of choice is truly amazing.

We were now entering the 23rd hour. After bidding farewell to our new friends at the park, we headed back to Wyckoff, where this year's 24 Hours of Kindness had begun. We still had an entire box of donuts to hand out, but figured someone along the way would graciously accept them. We arrived back in town just after 7:30, and things were very quiet. Because it was a Saturday, many people were slow to get outside. As we coasted through a small residential neighborhood, we noticed a woman walking her dog. Bill looked at me and asked, "What do you think?"

"Sure, let's give it a try," I replied.

Rolling the window down, I gave my pitch one last time: "Good morning! My friends and I are finishing a 24-hour marathon of doing acts of kindness, and we're almost done. We have this box of donuts and just wanted to offer it to you!"

She flipped out. (In a good way.) This woman was without a doubt the most animated person we'd encountered. With pure elation she exclaimed, "Are you serious? This is just *awesome!* I can't believe it!" Her enthusiasm made me wonder if she'd already eaten a box of pastries.

Still bouncing with delight, she said, "Your timing is perfect! I have to go to my AA meeting this morning, and I can bring these to give out to everyone." Looking down at her dog, she announced, "This is Nikki!" Then, in a slightly lower tone she introduced herself: "I'm Sandy . . . and I'm one year . . . one year sober."

Opening the door, I jumped out and said, "That deserves a hug!" Her arms flew open as she pulled me in tight and embraced me in a way that I won't soon forget. With tears of joy in her eyes, she went on to tell us how she'd turned her life around. In addition to sobriety, she was rebuilding her relationship with her family, involved heavily with her church, and finally giving back to the community that she claimed she'd "taken so much from."

With 30 minutes left in our marathon, Sandy's story and infectious energy had reignited our spirits and given us the fuel to do one more spontaneous act. Just around the corner was a small Laundromat.

Grabbing a handful of cards that read YOU'VE BEEN TAGGED BY KINDNESS . . . PASS IT ON, we went in to perform our last kind deed of the day. Taping four quarters on top of each card, we then stuck them to a dozen different washing machines. This would be a great surprise for the next wave of customers.

Emotionally and physically, all of us were now feeling the effects of what had been a life-changing and enlightening day. But rather than finish this memorable occasion by simply going back to the hotel, we all agreed on a special place to commemorate our accomplishments: Nana's house. We knew that this would mean a lot to Bill, and after meeting Nana the day before, I could think of no kinder place to celebrate.

To no one's surprise, Nana met us in the driveway, proudly displaying her POWERED BY KINDNESS T-shirt. Soon, other family members came out of the house and listened as we told stories and recounted the highlights of our day. After one final group photo and a round of hugs, we agreed that it was time to head back to the hotel and get some rest. While Bill backed the van out of the driveway, there were tears in his eyes. Noticing this, Karen gently placed her hand on his shoulder. Bill's grandmother meant the world to him. And having dedicated this event to Pop and completed it with Nana by his side brought everything full circle. It was such a touching moment and the perfect ending to an extraordinary day.

Chapter 15

Everyday Heroes

When I was a kid I had many heroes. Most were in the form of cape-wearing or web-slinging conquerors of evil such as Batman, Spider-Man, and Superman. My childhood was spent watching them on TV or reading about their amazing powers in my comic books. I wanted to be just like them. I even created my own special costumes, which included crime-fighting utility belts. Because of this interest, my neighborhood was the safest in town.

In 1981, I traded in my homemade "Super-Mike" suit and Star Wars beach towel (which transformed into the perfect cape) for a fedora hat and six-foot-long bullwhip. I can still remember going to see *Raiders of the Lost Ark* at the movie theater that summer and discovering what I believed to be the *coolest* action hero ever—Indiana Jones. To this day I can picture myself pretending to be Indy, zigzagging frantically through the fields behind my house. To the neighbors peering out their windows, it looked as if I was running away from a swarm of angry bees. But in my reality, I was dodging poisonous darts from the blowguns of South American jungle natives!

Eventually, it was considered uncool by my peers to have a bullwhip clipped to my belt, so I retired yet another hero of mine. Interestingly enough, I traded Indiana in for a new idol, who hailed from the state with the very same name. For ten years I lived, breathed, and bled Boston Celtic green by way of French Lick, Indiana's, very own Larry Bird. His brilliance on the basketball court is legendary, hence his nickname Larry Legend. And when he retired in 1992, you'd think my best friend had just died.

Much has changed since then. As I've grown spiritually over the past several years, I've noticed that great souls such as Jesus, Buddha, Mother Teresa, Gandhi, and Martin Luther King, Jr., have replaced the childhood celebrities and athletes that I once looked up to. Although these enlightened beings are no longer physically here, their spirits and timeless wisdom continue to have a profound impact on the world.

I'm very fortunate to have another hero in my life who has been with me from the very beginning. Even though I've spent 43 years with her, it took me a while to recognize this person as my greatest teacher. She's inspiring, positive, kind, loving, hysterically funny . . . and everything that's right with the world. And as with my other spiritual superheroes, time and again it has been her unconditional love that rescues me from the darkness whenever I'm lost.

My mother is my greatest hero. At the age of 63, she continues to amaze me with all she does and the grace with which she does it. Despite the fact that she rises each morning in tremendous pain due to chronic fibromyalgia, my mother never complains or feels sorry for herself. Even on days when she can barely walk because her body hurts so much, she pushes through incomprehensible discomfort and tells the world, "Today is going to be an awesome day!" And she means it. There's nothing phony about her attitude. My mom always sees the glass as half-full, recognizing and appreciating the gifts that each day offers.

I recently took my mom out for the day to visit

one of her favorite places—Boothbay Harbor. This quaint coastal town in Maine is her ideal spot to go for a day of shopping and lunch. Being near the ocean is truly my mother's version of heaven on Earth. If there were one place where she feels closest to God, I'm quite sure she'd say that it's along the sandy beaches that hug our rocky coastline. I'd have to agree with her perspective. There's something magical about being in the presence of such power and beauty, and I'm very fortunate to live only a few miles from the sea. But Mom, who lives in central Maine, has to travel quite a distance to smell the salty air. So to spend a day in such a beautiful setting was a real treat for her . . . oh yeah, and I brought Mollie along, too!

Telling my wife that I was going for a two-hour drive to take my mom to Boothbay Harbor for the day, *and* that I was bringing Mollie, prompted the reply: "Are you crazy?" Upon seeing her reaction, I thought for a moment, *Hmm . . . maybe I am.* Sometimes I forget how spirited Mollie can be when she goes to a new place. And, being a summer destination, this would offer ample opportunities for her to knock down a few innocent tourists or, at the very least, pull me off a dock at the first sight of a passing lobster boat. But Cara's question backfired when it sparked another thought, ensuring that Mollie would definitely be going with me. Sure, I wanted to have a relaxing day with my mom, but hey, I'm a writer, and I thought bringing Mollie along could potentially create some good material for my book!

I could see my mother was overjoyed when I picked her up that morning. We'd been talking about this trip for weeks, and she was raring to go. Even though it was still early, she already had her wacky sense of humor fired up. When I asked her if she brought extra clothes in case it rained, she replied, "Michael, I *always* bring a change of clothing. I'm 63! One big sneeze, and I could pee my pants!" I almost did exactly that after her comment. My mom is truly one of the classiest ladies you'd ever meet, but she's also one of the funniest. And when we get together, we love to laugh.

Rolling into town, both Mollie and my mother sat up straight like two excited kids, each pressing their nose against the window as we passed the gift shops and restaurants lining the streets. While they continued to take in the sights, I scanned both sides of the road looking for a place to park. Noticing my search, my mom exclaimed, "Here, take this! Give your old mother a good spot so we won't have to walk so far." Looking down, I saw she was holding her handicap-parking pass. Because Mom is always so upbeat, I often forget that she has a hard time getting around. Physically she may struggle, but her spirit outshines most people half her age.

Based on our plans for the day, we hit the jackpot of parking spots right in the center of town. The location couldn't have been more perfect. Smiling, Mom piped up, "See, hanging out with an old lady has its benefits!" She started gathering a few things to take while I climbed in the backseat with Mollie, going through my checklist: dog cookies, two poop bags, harness, leash, water . . . and a whole bunch of patience. I closed the side door to go around back and open the hatch before letting Mollie out. Mom jumped out of the front seat at the same time, stepped onto the curb, reached for something on the side of the door—and that's when I heard a sound so nerve-racking, so awful, and so frightening that it made my knees turn to jelly. *Click!* My mother's words said it all: "Uh oh!" as we both stood outside looking at each other while Mollie remained in the car.

I frantically began to dig through my pockets. "No way. Oh, come on . . . where are they?!" I tried not to panic, but as Mollie stared at me from behind the locked doors, I knew we were in trouble. I had screwed up big time. My mother wanted to take the blame for hitting the lock button, but it was totally my fault. I was the one who left the keys in the backseat, where they now lay resting under my confused dog's tail. She looked back at me like we were in one of those scary Scooby-Doo movies where Scooby looks at Shaggy and says, "Ruh-roh, Raggy!"

Two hours from home and the spare keys, no AAA auto service, and the forecast for the day was humid and 90 degrees. I stood there in a daze, repeating the words, "What am I going to do? How do I get her out?"

Thank God my mother is always coolheaded about things. As I started to freak, she kept saying, "Don't worry. Everything will be fine . . . we'll get her out."

"How?" I asked.

"We'll find a police officer or somebody to help us." Her words calmed me down. I took in a few deep breaths and decided to go look for anyone who might be able to unlock the car door.

Racing down the sidewalk, I peered into the windows of the high-end gift shops and art galleries. For whatever reason, I decided not to stop and ask the people inside for help; something kept me moving forward. I really didn't know who or what I was even looking for, but it just felt like there had to be a solution to our problem nearby. Passing a dozen or so shops, I finally came to the end of the street where only one store remained: Two Salty Dogs Pet Outfitters. Lying beside the entrance were two beautiful black Labs. The one closest to me looked up as if to say, *Hey, we heard what happened. Come inside, and we'll help you figure this whole thing out.*

As I walked into the store, a tall, jovial man greeted me from behind the counter. "Hey, how are you? What can I help you find today?" His friendly tone put me at ease.

I wanted to reply, "Good morning, I'm a dumbass tourist!" but instead what came out of my mouth was, "Hi there . . . I just did something kind of dumb and was hoping you could help me. I sort of locked my keys, and my dog, in my car."

Without hesitation, he smiled and said, "Oh, that's no problem at all! I'll just call Vick for you."

I wanted to hug him. "Seriously, you have someone that unlocks doors around here?"

"Sure," he said. "It happens all the time." Did I mention I wanted to hug him?

After placing the call, the store owner told me Vick would arrive in a matter of minutes. When I stepped outside to wait for him, I could see in the distance that my mother was still standing beside the car keeping an eye on Mollie. I called her cell phone to deliver the good news. "We're all set, Mom! A guy will be here soon to unlock the doors." I then thought of something: "Mom . . . is Mollie in the front seat or the back?"

"Well, she was in the back, but she just jumped in front a minute ago."

With trepidation I asked, "Uh, aren't those two-pound date bars you bought in the front seat?"

"Well yes, but she wouldn't eat those, would she?"

"Ma, did you forget? She eats sewing needles and CDs! You've got to go around and tap on the windows. Do whatever it takes to get her in the backseat again!"

I was standing a quarter of a mile from where the car was parked, but even at that distance it was a comical scene. While still on the phone, my mother was knocking on the back window, saying, "Moooooollie! Moooooollie! Come here! Get in the backseat, girl. Don't you eat my date bar!" My mom had been raving about "the world's best date bars" all morning. She knew I loved them as a kid, so she bought two from Dysart's, a popular truck stop and diner near her house. It took some convincing, but it finally worked; Mollie was now in the backseat where she belonged—sitting on my keys.

When Vick pulled up in front of the store, I was ecstatic. Rolling down his window, he grinned and said, "You the guy who locked his dog in his car?"

Laughing, I replied, "Yeah, that's me." I was so grateful for his arrival. I pointed to the end of the street and told him I'd meet him there. When I finally got to my car, he'd already sprung into action. Within seconds, he emptied a canvas pouch filled with cool gadgets. Two minutes later, *click*—the door was open! Like a superhero, he'd saved my dog and the day! In a flash, he then placed his tools back into the bag, hopped into the Vickmobile, and drove away. It was the best $20 I've ever spent.

Now with all of the drama behind us, we could begin our day. The three of us began a leisurely stroll through the downtown area. Actually, Mom was strolling; I, however, was rolling—as in, rolling down the hill! Within the first ten minutes, Mollie had already tripped me three times due to her zigzagging all over the sidewalk. Whenever there is a lot of activity and new things to smell, she drags me down the street. (Sort of like what happens on trash day.) Even her so-called Easy Walk Harness doesn't help. Fifteen minutes later, my arm felt like it was going to fall off, and my mother could see that I was clearly stressed from Mollie's incessant pulling. Looking at her, I finally said, "Ma, let's go to the pet store for a minute. I want to thank the guy who helped me and see if he sells harnesses."

Walking through the door, Mollie did what she always does when we enter a pet store—she went totally nuts. Between the wall of stuffed toys and the baskets filled with bones, rawhides, and other dog chews, her senses went wild . . . and so did she! The owner looked up, noticing that I had my hands full. After Mollie pulled me across the store, knocking every item from the first shelf onto the floor, I looked at him and said, "I'll give you $1,000 if you can fix this problem!" Every customer in the store turned and looked at my dog as if she were a circus freak.

The owner said with confidence, "I've got just the thing, and it will only cost you $27.99."

I didn't believe him. I'd already tried several leashes and harnesses over the years, but nothing ever worked. They just made her slightly more "manageable." But I figured that I had nothing to lose at this point. My only other option was carrying her all day.

The man pulled out what looked like a piece of rope with a metal ring attached to it. "This is the Weiss Walkie," he informed me. I watched as he clipped it to Mollie's collar, slid the rest of the rope underneath her belly, and ran the other end through the metal ring. When he gently pulled on the handle, a miracle happened: Mollie stayed still. She stood tall, looking almost regal. Handing me the leash, he said, "Here, take her for a walk and see what happens."

I thought I'd died and gone to heaven. It felt like someone had just waved a magic wand over my dog. My mom kept looking at us in amazement as Mollie pranced down the road like a princess. Although I do believe in miracles, I thought that I would witness world peace before my dog would walk in a straight line. Somewhere, pigs were flying, and hell most definitely had just frozen over.

I hurried back into the store and couldn't get my wallet out fast enough. "You just changed my life," I let the store owner know.

He smiled back at me and said, "I thought that might do the trick!" Like my feelings toward Vick just 30 minutes prior, I now loved this guy, too. I just kept looking at him with total awe and appreciation. I wanted to wrap my arms around him, but the wide counter didn't offer me the opportunity. This man was now another hero to me. It was beginning to feel like the town of Boothbay Harbor was filled with canine-saving crusaders.

With one hand on the new leash and a pen in the other, I leaned forward to sign the credit card slip for the most glorious purchase I'd ever made. Even the

$20 I'd spent for Vick's help earlier now paled in comparison. But seconds later, pigs must have been crashing to the ground. Evidently, I forgot to read the fine print on the Weiss Walkie, which surely must have said: "This product is for walking purposes only and will not stop your dog from seeing the entire world as her own personal buffet." I'd neglected to consider the extra freedom this new leash gave her, because it was two feet longer than her old one.

With both paws now up on the counter, Mollie stuck her entire face into the complimentary dog-cookie bowl. I quickly pushed her back and asked my mother to take the leash while I paid for my purchase. But Mom's strength was no match for a hungry poodle. Mollie lunged back up to the counter, knocking business cards and brochures to the floor. Within seconds, the entire bowl of snacks was empty, leaving only a few crumbs. Customers in the store looked on as I screamed, "Mollie, get down!" As her paws hit the floor, she immediately noticed a basket near my feet filled with tasty rawhide lamb ears. Having just enough slack on the end of the leash, she buried her entire face into the basket in search of just the right one.

They say that life will often give you the same scenarios again and again if you don't learn your lesson the first time. I now wholeheartedly believed this philosophy to be true. Otherwise, why else would Mollie clamp down on a piece of rawhide at the *very* moment I decided to stick my fingers into her mouth? It was no chicken bone like the last time, but the result was pretty much the same. Once I was able to free the lamb ear (and my thumb) from her clenched jaw, I looked down to see the familiar sight of red oozing from my hand. I swear I heard a little voice say, "I told you so."

As we headed out the door, I started to laugh. "Can you believe that I'm writing a book about her?" I asked my mother.

She laughed, too, and replied, "Poor Mollie. You've had a rough morning."

Glancing down at my black-and-blue thumb, I thought, *It's been no picnic for me, either!*

Nevertheless, it was still early, and I was going to do everything I could to ensure that we'd enjoy this day. And we did—especially since the new, hot-pink leash I was holding was now working like a dream. (Hey, she's a girl, and I knew my wife would love it.) Now we were able to walk peacefully through town, have lunch without any catastrophes, and make tons of new friends.

The day was supposed to be about my mom, but as usual Mollie stole the show. Everyone wanted to stop and meet her. And once I mentioned that she was the subject of a new book, adults and children alike wanted their pictures taken with her.

We had a relaxing lunch on the fishing docks, and then I decided to take my mom to the other side of town where the scenery was even more spectacular. We found a winding coastal road that offered a perfect view of the ocean and ample opportunities for pictures. When we pulled over, Mom got out and went crazy with her camera. I got out, too, but decided Mollie would be fine in the car for five minutes. It touched my heart deeply to see my mother so happy. She was in bliss photographing the water, islands, and beautiful homes that surrounded us. Then I thought that it would be nice to have a photo of the three of us in this spot so I could remember our special day. When I began walking to the car to let Mollie out . . . I couldn't see her anywhere. The backseat was empty, which could only mean one thing!

"Mom! Where did you leave the date bars?"

Unperturbed, she said, "They're on the floor in front of my seat."

Not anymore!

Rushing to the passenger-side door, I could see Mollie's butt sticking straight up in the air. When I opened the door, she looked up with her snout covered in sugar, dates, and oats. An entire bar, its packaging, and even the Dysart's sticker were all gone. After pulling Mollie out of the car, my mom examined the crime scene; her seat was covered in gooey remnants while the sweet scent of dates filled the air. Trying not to laugh, she turned to me and said, "Please tell me she ate *your* date bar and not mine."

We lost it. People walking by must have thought we were insane as we stood in the road, doubled over from laughing so hard. It was one of those mother-and-son moments that are unforgettable. It also re-iterated the heart of the conversation we had during our drive to the coast that morning. My mom and I had a very deep discussion about being positive. The truth is that she hasn't had an easy life. A very difficult childhood combined with a 20-year marriage to my father—who all but destroyed her self-esteem—had taken their toll on her. But she's no quitter. Eventually, she was able to pick up the pieces of her life; meet my kindhearted stepfather; and rediscover her brilliant, beautiful self.

"Mom, you're always so happy. How do you stay positive all the time?"

Without missing a beat, she answered, "I learned years ago that loving yourself is where it all begins.

Sure, I may look older and feel broken down sometimes, but I've never been happier with myself. I like who I am. I also don't take life too seriously anymore—even when I don't feel good, I try my best to stay positive and have fun. But I think the biggest reason I'm so happy now is because I no longer focus on the past or worry about the future. I now live in the present and see each moment as a gift. Even something as simple as eating breakfast or drinking my first cup of coffee makes me feel grateful. It took me years to realize this, but it's the little things that matter the most." Her response reminded me once again why she is my greatest hero.

After dropping her off, I headed home thinking about the events of the day. Between Vick, the door-opening magician; the pet-shop owner eliminating my walking woes; friendly locals giving me directions; and the saving grace of my optimistic mother, it felt as if I'd been rescued many times over—which is a reminder that anyone can be a hero. Granted, a caped crusader will always sell more movie tickets than everyday gestures of love, but maybe in real life helping those in need is the first step toward saving the world.

That day was also a reminder that serving others is only one side of the coin. Without receiving kindness from others, there can be no giving. This is another clue to mastering Mollie's wisdom. She's never once said no to a pat on the head, a hug from a child, or even a simple praise of "Good girl!" She simply takes it all in with gratitude.

A few miles before arriving home, the sky went pitch-black. Webs of electricity lit up the highway, followed by violent cracks of thunder. High winds shook the car. In the rearview mirror I could see Mollie anxiously sitting upright. As the storm intensified, she pressed her body against my seat in an effort to be closer to me. Reaching back, I placed my hand on her head, gently massaging her ears while saying, "It's okay, girl. Don't worry, everything's going to be okay."

Cape or no cape, in that moment, and in Mollie's eyes . . . I was the hero.

Chapter 16

Learning to Love Again

I recently had the chance to visit a friend whom I hadn't seen in quite a while. Mike was like a little brother to me, and, at one time, my best fishing buddy. After getting to know his parents many years ago and learning of Mike's passion for angling, I started taking him with me whenever I went out in my boat. From his freshman year right up until he graduated high school, the two of us spent countless days on lakes and ponds in Maine in search of trophy bass.

After graduation, Mike made the decision to leave home and join the Army. I wasn't especially crazy about this idea, since things in Iraq were intensifying, and the thought of his leaving with so much uncertainty had me scared for his life. But despite my subtle hints for us to open a bait-and-tackle shop together, he still left for basic training, ended up going to war . . . and came home a changed man.

Mike has been to hell and back and witnessed more suffering in a day than you and I will see in a lifetime. Those who haven't served in this capacity could never begin to understand what he's been through. Two tours in Iraq, multiple life-threatening injuries, losing best friends, and being surrounded by violence and death for years are only a small glimpse of what he experienced. He may be home, but the battle has not ended. In addition to recurring nightmares, he continues to be reminded of the horrors of war through the emotional and physical wounds he sustained.

On the morning we met for coffee, which happened to be September 11, Mike looked really good. Cara and I had attended his wedding a year earlier, and I could see that married life was agreeing with him. As we sat down, he began by saying, "I remember 9/11 was just like this—a perfect fall day. The sky was so blue. The temperature was the same, too."

Doing the math, I said, "Man, you were just a sophomore in high school."

"Yeah, I remember every detail of that morning. I had Latin class, first period. My teacher was late because he hit a deer on the way to school. So we were all sitting in the classroom waiting, and I said, 'Screw it. I'm gonna turn the TV on.' And when I flipped through the channels, the news was on every station showing a plane hitting the first tower. When my teacher walked in, he asked what happened; and I said some pilot must have messed up, fell asleep, or something. Next thing I know, the second plane came in, and I said, 'Holy shit, it's going down. We're being attacked!' So I left school, went home, and told my parents to take me to the Army recruiting center that day."

After a long swig of coffee, he continued, "9/11 sealed the deal for me. I spent days watching the footage over and over again. Seeing clips of the planes, the people jumping from the buildings, and the sounds of bodies hitting the ground fueled my anger and prepared me for going to war."

Echoing his statement, I said, "We were all angry after it happened. None of us will ever be the same after that day."

Nodding in agreement, Mike replied, "Nope. Never. In my mind, that was our Pearl Harbor."

Eventually, we got into general conversation about house projects and tales of Mike's recent fishing trips. He then talked about his new dog, whom he adored but who also drove him crazy. "Some days I want to choke her, while others I just hug her tight." Taking in this new addition to his family had been a difficult transition. She was replacing his best pal, his dog Boston, who had died the year before. Boston meant everything to Mike. He was a true friend, a constant companion, loyal, and especially unconditionally loving. This amazing pet brought tremendous healing to his owner's life after he came home from the war. Boston's ability to tune in to Mike's energy and respond in empathetic ways was unlike anything a human being could offer. Just his presence alone made a huge difference.

When I first expressed my condolences for my friend's loss, his words back to me were both heartbreaking and haunting: "Losing Boston almost put me over the edge. Seriously, I didn't think I was going to make it."

I said, "What do you mean?"

"Fourteen of my friends died in Iraq, and I just couldn't handle another big loss. It was one too many. The day that I had to put Boston down, I couldn't speak. I didn't say a word to anyone. It was as if I lost my mom or another person in my life. When I was finally alone in the house, I locked myself in the bathroom with my gun."

Hearing this made my heart feel as if it stopped beating. I was in shock. And while his big blue eyes gazed up and away, my own began to fill with tears. Choking up, I finally said, "Mike, does your wife know this?"

Turning, and now looking straight at me, he replied, "I've never told anyone that before . . . just you."

I had chills. After a few seconds of silence, I asked, "So what happened? I mean, what stopped you?"

"It was too easy. Anybody can kill himself. And I thought about my guys in Iraq—the ones dead and the ones still alive. If they'd been with me, they would have smacked me in the head and told me: 'Suck it the fuck up. Shit happens. You lost 14 guys, and Boston was just another one.' Yeah, I knew they'd be pissed at me. So I guess it wasn't the right place or the right time."

After discussing Boston for several minutes, Mike began to open up even more. He spoke specifically about having little or no compassion for others. His frustration with the human race had peaked, and there was now a fortress around his heart. "I'm sorry, but I just can't stand people anymore!" His eyes, normally bright and clear, were now darkened with intensity. "I'm tired of everybody whining and complaining about their life. They have no clue what a bad day *really* looks like."

I know Mike well enough to emphatically state that he is truly one of the most honest, caring, funny, and loyal friends I've ever known. But he's human. He's also had to experience things that you and I couldn't even begin to comprehend. Our conversation had me concerned about his well-being, but I had to agree with him—most people, including me, tend to complain and get bent out of shape over ridiculous things. While others are bitching because they received mustard on their sandwich when they wanted mayo, there's a kid in a blazing-hot desert dodging bullets and fighting for our freedom. Mike had come home to see just how out of touch our culture could be. There was no arguing his point. Too often we take our lives and independence for granted and forget how blessed we are.

Lighting up a cigarette, he went on, "I just wish everyone could understand how good they have it here and what our guys go through. I see all these people put yellow-ribbon magnets on their cars and then think they're supporting our troops, and I appreciate that, but they just don't see the whole picture."

I asked him, "What would you want them to know?"

He replied sharply, "Details—the minute-by-minute, thought-by-thought process of what it looks like, sounds like, smells like, and tastes like. Then maybe more Americans would step up and do everything they can to help our guys when we come back. The more that people understand, the more willing they might be to help our troops."

And there it was again—the buzzword of my summer: *understanding.* For several months I'd been hearing it over and over from John; now it was Mike who was helping me realize how powerful this word is. Curious, but not wanting to cross a line, I posed the question, "If there was one experience, one event that if people only knew about would completely shake them to the core and help them understand what you guys have to go through, what would it be?"

As we leaned on the tailgate of his pickup, Mike looked down, paused briefly, and then replied, "The day John was killed: December 23, two days before Christmas."

Upset with myself, I thought, *What the hell are you thinking? You shouldn't have asked a question like that.* But it was soon evident that Mike wanted to share the story of losing his friend.

"All hell broke loose that day. It seemed like everyone had congregated and decided to try and wipe us off the face of the earth, but we let loose on them. It was a dogfight all day, all night, and into the next morning. It was fucking bad. Then early in the morning of the 23rd, John, who was the gunner on the tank, got a message out that we needed ammo. When the ammo arrived, I jumped up on the hull of the tank and was helping them load it. John was just two or three feet away from me in the commander's hole, and I kept passing him rounds. Then I handed him the last box of .50 caliber, and that's when a mortar came down. It came in from the back, and . . ."

Mike paused for what felt like an eternity. His gaze seemed frozen in time as he stared at the pile of scrap wood in the back of his truck. Finally, he looked up and continued. "The blast shook me, but I didn't get hit. I was just out of the way. John was facing the other way, though . . . and . . . it . . . it took three-quarters of his head off. All I felt was the rush of the explosion and being hit by pieces of his body. I was sprayed with his blood, and I got hit with his skull fragments. I fell straight off the tank, but John plunged straight back in. He died instantly. I had to pull him out and put him in a body bag." He paused again before saying, "So that's why I don't do Christmas anymore."

Wiping tears away with my shirtsleeve, I looked down, and that's when I noticed his license plate for the first time: "Purple Heart, Combat Wounded." And then Mike summed up my original question by saying, "So that's just one experience that might open people's eyes."

I agreed and told him, "That one is more than enough, buddy."

"Maybe. But like I said before, I just wish others could understand. I mean, so many of us are struggling to readjust here as civilians. The PTSD, nightmares, depression, rage—all of the bullshit that we bring home with us."

After a final drag from his cigarette, Mike flicked its remains into a sewer drain. In an attempt to change the subject, I told him about the book I was writing and how its premise was loving everyone. Mike said, "I know this may sound strange, but I really don't know how to totally love people anymore, you know, like the way they deserve to be. I think it's the result of my training and the experiences I had in Iraq. It's just not in my emotional range now. It's gone."

He went on to explain how the wall he'd built up was affecting his relationships, and so I asked him, "Was the wall there before you left and fought in the war?"

"No. It wasn't even there early on in Iraq. When I was with the guys over there, we were like a band of brothers, even closer than family. I mean, when you're willing to give your life for someone, that's beyond love. It's eternal. But then there comes a day when you see a brother die, and another, and then another. Eventually you shut off the part of you that loves. I mean, you keep the bond, the trust, the friendship, and all of that stuff; but because it hurts so badly to lose someone, you do your best not to put yourself in that situation again."

I asked, "Are you getting help? Have you been seeing a counselor?"

"I tried, but nothing worked. They don't understand me. There is only one thing that helps me feel any peace and calms me down."

This made me think that perhaps he had been exploring spirituality or had even started going to church. I soon discovered that in a way, he had. Not in the traditional sense, mind you, but he had found a place that allowed him to heal his mind, body, and soul. Most of all, this temple allowed him to give and receive what he felt he was lacking most—unconditional love.

Animal therapy has been Mike's saving grace. Working at local shelters and caring for a variety of God's critters has been the key to keeping his heart open. But as helpful as this has been for him, it has had an even greater impact on those he works with. Mike has a gift. His ability to connect, understand, and sense what an animal is feeling is awe inspiring—especially when it comes to dogs. When I asked how it came so naturally to him, he explained that breaking the rules was the first step. "During the classes I took on working with dogs, they told me to never make eye contact or stare, because it would only make them nervous, even aggressive. But honestly, I do the opposite. I always look into their eyes so I can read them. I see their expression, the little twitches in their nose, everything about their face. They also stare back at me. And because of what I went through, they pick up on my animal instinct. Without even saying a word, they can hear me. They have that sixth sense, you know. I tell them with my eyes that I want to help them and be their friend. Sometimes it takes hours, sometimes days, but I've never had a dog that didn't eventually surrender."

A few weeks back, he proved this through the work he was doing with a rescued pit bull. When the dog arrived at the shelter, his skin was so raw and shredded that Mike said it looked as if someone had sprayed bullets into his body. Sadly, these markings were the result of illegal dogfighting. The staff warned that this animal was dangerous, and getting close to him would be impossible. The angry dog spent hours each day attacking the front of his cage. At one point, the staff considered putting him down. They said that he was simply too vicious and a danger to everyone at the shelter. Mike, however, felt differently. Barging in on a meeting that he was not authorized to attend, he yelled, "Don't touch this dog! I know I can get through to him!" It took some convincing, but they finally agreed to give my gifted friend an opportunity to work with one of the worst cases of animal abuse they'd ever seen.

What the staff thought would take weeks took only days. Everyone was shocked. After three days, Mike was able to open the door. By the end of the week, he was in the cage. And by the following week, Mike had earned enough trust to be able to hold the once-brutal dog like a timid puppy.

In awe of this amazing feat, I exclaimed, "How was this even possible? Mike, this dog could have turned on you at any given moment. He could have killed you!"

After taking a long drag from his newly lit cigarette, he responded, "It's all about energy. I only approached him with calm, controlled, assertive energy. But the biggest reason is that we understood each other. He knew I was like him. I'd been to war, too—we'd both been wounded in battle."

Moved by his words, I told him, "Mike, this tells me that you're learning to love again; you're tearing down that wall."

Looking back at me with a slight grin, he replied, "Maybe that's true. Yeah, maybe one brick at a time."

That evening, just as the sun was going down, Cara and I took Mollie for a walk. As we wandered through the neighborhood, we both noticed the silence that surrounded us. "This is just the way it was on that night 11 years ago," I said. "It was so quiet, hardly any traffic at all; everyone was inside glued to the TV." I then told her about my conversation with Mike from that morning, explaining to her how he'd shared his worst moments from the war, his emotional struggles, and his recent experience of taming a pit bull.

She was quiet for a while and then finally asked, "Why do you think some people can move forward and love again after a tragedy, but not others?"

Her question made me think of a quote that I keep on my desk from *A Course in Miracles:* "Your task is not to seek for love, but merely to seek and find all of the barriers within yourself that you have built against it."

Compared to Mike, most of us have had it easy. Still, no one is immune to suffering. We all feel pain. We all build walls. And at one time or another, we're all learning to love again.

Chapter 17

Enlightenment

"So what do you think enlightenment is like?" I asked.

As usual, John was sitting up straight and tall, a posture he often refers to as "losing the back of your chair." Smiling at me, he responded, "First of all, try to recognize that this idea of enlightenment is not something that just happens. Someone can't just bop you on the head, and *poof!* you're done." Laughing at his own words, he continued by saying, "It's much more like exercise or working out."

"So it's a process?"

"Yes, absolutely. And the more you practice, the more understanding and wisdom you will have.

This wisdom is what will bring you closer to being awakened."

John went on to explain how a Buddha is not one person but rather a nature that is within everyone. "Enlightenment is available to each of us. And to accomplish this, you have to first understand that a Buddha has three bodies, which are called *dharmakaya, sambhogakaya,* and *nirmanakaya."* Beginning with dharmakaya, John explained that this means seeing the infinite possibilities in all things: "As you experience higher levels of consciousness, everything and everyone is recognized as having unlimited potential. No limits. Having this wisdom allows you to instantly change your negative perception of a person or thing into something pure and good. It's like flipping a switch."

Next, he described sambhogakaya: "This is when you begin to see beauty and goodness in all things. Criticism disappears. Everything and everyone makes you happy."

At this point, I had a question: "So does this mean we become totally free from judgment?"

"Yes. Nothing offends you, because you now have deeper understandings. This allows you to recognize every person, yourself, and all objects as good."

"Is this consistent; I mean, does it fade or will it always be this way?"

Smiling back at me, John answered, "Well, I'm not enlightened yet, but I believe that it will be a very, very high level of happiness. To put it mildly, bliss."

Finally, John described the third Buddha body, nirmanakaya, saying, "This is where you really want to be—you are in a constant state of mindfulness, sending out thoughts of happiness to all. This is also when a Buddha puts everything he or she knows into action, radiating love, compassion, kindness, and great joy to all sentient beings. You become like Jesus, who was a great bodhisattva."

Seeing my expression of curiosity, he continued, "A *bodhisattva* is one who is motivated to attain enlightenment not just for him- or herself, but for all. This is where you become a gift to the world, helping *everyone* to awaken."

I could have listened to John talk about Buddhism all day. He had painted a beautiful picture for me of what spiritual illumination would look like. In his easygoing way, he finished the lesson with, "So, that's a general idea of how it all works—the three Buddha bodies and enlightenment. Sound good?"

Enthusiastically, I said, "I'll take it. Count me in!"

With a slightly serious tone, he added, "Then you *have* to continue meditating. This will allow you to get beyond your thoughts and labels and realize that they aren't who you are. Anger, impatience, even cravings, for example—these are only human conditions, sort of like having a cold. They just come and go."

"And what should I do if I get stuck or have a hard time moving past negative thoughts?"

"It's okay. This is all part of the process. When you start going down a certain road of negativity, or you make a mistake, just stop and recognize it as a situation that has to be dealt with. It's not a big deal. It happens all the time. Don't immediately judge it or yourself; just give the situation a little space so you can have a better understanding. Sometimes we need to step back, relax, and breathe through things so we can see clearly."

I took John's words to heart. Enlightenment itself didn't appear to be on the horizon anytime soon, but I had definitely "enlightened up" and was no longer stressing about my writing, family issues, my neighbor, or other petty concerns. My ability to feel peaceful was most evident on the days I practiced *metta,* a meditation in which thoughts of loving-kindness are sent out to myself, those I know, strangers, the difficult people in my life, and then all sentient beings. At first, sending love and kindness toward those individuals who pushed my buttons wasn't easy, but after a friend told me the following parable, I had a whole new perspective:

> Legend has it that there was once a great spiritual teacher who had discovered a large and potentially dangerous snake living in his room. Each morning when he awoke and turned on the light, he saw it slip away under a storage cabinet. He didn't want to harm it, so he decided that perhaps leaving the door open would encourage it to depart. This went on for many days, but the reluctant reptile was still unwilling to leave. For almost an entire week they lived together. Knowing that this species was venomous, the master simply did his best not to scare the snake or make it feel intimidated by his presence.
>
> Finally, one evening as he was sitting in meditation, the master spoke to the snake quietly in his mind, through metta. "Dear friend, it's not that I dislike you, wish you harm, or harbor any ill feelings toward you, but our minds work differently. And because we're experiencing a dissimilar consciousness right now, it would be easy for a misunderstanding to occur between us. The fields are quite beautiful this time of the year and offer many places where you can be in peace without the anxiety of living with me. I truly want you to

be happy, healthy, free from suffering, and full of peace in your life."

This went on for several minutes, as he sent thoughts of kindness and well wishes to the snake. The master finally opened his eyes at the end of his meditation only to see the large reptile come out from hiding and slither out the door, never to be seen again.

Because the idea of loving everyone can feel daunting at times, this story has helped me to appreciate that love, in the traditional sense, isn't always the best choice. If the teacher had tried to get close to the snake, hold it, or offer it affection, the outcome could have been disastrous. Sometimes good intentions can go a long way. And metta is an effective way to do this.

On most days, this meditation plants a seed of peace in my mind, reinvigorating my power of choice, perspective, and attitude of how I see the world. Realizing that life is not happening to me, but rather, *I am happening to life,* changes everything. That being said, there are still days when I completely miss the mark and hope that, like the snake, the difficult people in my life will slither away, never to return. But now, when those darker thoughts do arise, I try not to beat myself up. I still have more inner work to do, but, thanks to John, I'm beginning to *understand*.

John's description of enlightenment and the three Buddha bodies now had me even more convinced of Mollie's divinity. Viewing her as a Buddha may seem unconventional, but it's hard to deny the similarities between her and a spiritual master. She recognizes infinite possibilities in everyone and everything, is free from judgment, only sees goodness in others, and consistently exudes pure love and joy. These are Buddha-like and undeniably Christ-like qualities. I've even found myself in a few challenging situations where I asked, "What would Mollie do? Would she judge, shun, resent, be unauthentic, and so on . . . or instead choose to love?" I'll admit, tackling life this way may not always be practical, but whenever I make a decision from this perspective, it tends to create happiness for others and for me.

I was recently working in Washington, D.C., when I met a man who emulated the traits of a true bodhisattva. His jovial personality actually reminded me of the Dalai Lama, who once said, "I try to treat every person I meet like an old friend, and that gives me a real sensation of happiness." But instead of wearing a flowing orange robe, this sage donned a crisp, black-and-white uniform while carrying a tray of food to my hotel room. Before my dinner even made it inside, his spirit burst through the door: "*Ohhh mon,* look at you eating so healthy. You know how to pick good food! Is this how I can get a flat stomach like yours?" His exuberance and thick accent made me smile. Amused by his comments, I thanked him and asked him to come in.

His name was Kimani. I soon found out that he was from Jamaica and had been living in the U.S. for many years. Setting the tray of food on the table, he inquired again, "So do you always eat so good, my friend?"

"I do my best, but it's not always easy when I travel."

Still beaming, Kimani replied, "Oh yes, so much sugar in this country! I cannot believe how the children eat so badly. They also should not drink soda; it is so very bad for them."

Curious about his feelings on this subject, I asked, "So what is the solution? How do we get kids to change?"

Not missing a beat, he responded with, "As I tell my children time after time, you must embrace responsibility. Only *you* can make your life great!"

Agreeing with his perspective, I remarked, "And that's what makes you a responsible parent."

"Yes. All I can do is live in good ways and hope

216

my children will follow. But once they go out the door, they must be in charge and make the best choices."

"So why do you think so many kids do not make positive decisions?"

Kimani's answer could not have been more perfect: "People will never be healthy in their bodies or souls until they love themselves. Self-love always causes one to make responsible choices."

Upon hearing these inspiring words, I pointed at the chair to my left and said, "Please, sit down for a minute."

With noticeable trepidation, he lowered his voice as if the room were bugged. "I've never sat with a guest before. They could fire me for this." Placing a hand on his shoulder, I promised him it would be okay.

For the next 20 minutes, Kimani shared his insights. The passion and eye contact he displayed sent a clear message: *You are important to me, and I care about you.* I was particularly moved by his optimistic points of view. Whether he discussed politics in D.C. or global issues, he made it clear by saying more than once, "I still believe in humanity. There is goodness in everyone's heart."

Inspired by his words, I asked, "So what keeps

you feeling happy, Kimani? Something tells me that you're always this way." Chuckling wholeheartedly, he replied, "In the kitchen they call me 'peace and love'! They're joking with me, because I spend too much time with the people. But I just *love* the guests so much. I'll sometimes walk the grounds looking for anyone who appears to be alone. I see many lost souls here, very rich and powerful men, but so empty on the inside. They go down to the river in front of the hotel just to stare at the water. So I find them. And when I do, I just listen. Sometimes all a man needs is for someone to hear him." Kimani paused, and then he answered my question: "Yes, that is most definitely it. The people. That is what brings me the most happiness."

And there it was. It was astounding . . . and humbling. The answer I'd been looking for all summer had been delivered alongside my now-lukewarm meal. For months I had been learning and practicing methods so I could love others more deeply. But Kimani's answer had revealed the other side of the coin. It also brought John's words back to life from an earlier conversation when I asked him, "When someone becomes enlightened, will they automatically love everyone? Or does a person have to love everyone first to become enlightened?" His reply of

"It works both ways, brother" now totally resonated. After months of observing, pondering, writing, and trying to figure out what made Mollie tick, it finally made sense: *People are the trigger to her joy.* People are her meditation. People are her spiritual practice. And people are the primary reason she lives, loves, and is enlightened.

Chapter 18

The Long Walk Home

"Hey, Michael!" Hearing my name called out, Mollie and I turned to see a young man pedaling his bike across the road to greet me. "I loved your talk the other day. It was awesome. I tried to see you afterward, but there were too many people around you."

I had just visited a local high school a few days before. It was an experience that I'd been trying to forget. Unfortunately, a handful of kids had decided to act less than kind during one of the more sensitive parts of my presentation. While I was discussing my father's suicide and how it had forever changed the course of my life, a few students began talking loudly and acting disrespectful. Eventually, they were removed from the audience, but the damage had already been done.

After the young man parked his bike beside me, he said, "I'm really sorry about those noisy kids. They're always getting into trouble. I even went up to them at lunch and told them to grow up. Everybody in the school thinks they're jerks. But the biggest reason I wanted to talk to you the other day is because of what you said about your dad. It helped me so much."

I was moved by his sincerity and the fact that he had been able to take something away from my presentation. "What's your name, pal?"

"David," he said.

"First of all, David, thank you so much for taking the time to approach me. And as far as those guys who were interrupting, it happens sometimes. Just knowing that you were listening means a lot to me."

"I wasn't just listening. I was feeling every word you spoke—especially when you said you now view your father's death as an opportunity to help people instead of playing the victim. I almost cried when you said that."

Still unsure of the reason why it had touched such a nerve, I asked, "What made you feel that way?" Looking down at the handlebars of his bike, he slowly replied, "Because my uncle just committed suicide. He was more like a dad to me than my actual father. And when he died, I didn't think anyone understood what losing someone that way feels like. But after hearing your story . . . I knew you did."

This gave me a whole new perspective when it comes to speaking at schools. Before meeting David, I was wrapped up in the idea that I needed to connect with every single person in the auditorium. Now I realize that if 1 out of 1,000 people is positively affected, I've made a difference. To change one life is to change the world. And what David didn't realize is that he just changed mine. Because of his bravery and openness toward me, I no longer felt as if my words had fallen on deaf ears.

After I thanked David and shook his hand, Mollie and I continued on our journey. Looking down, I noticed that the sidewalks were littered with one of my favorite natural creations—leaves. To me, the most spectacular thing about October in New England is its color. Each fall, as the trees transform into a vibrant array of red, orange, yellow, and gold, it's like watching Mother Nature set off silent fireworks. As Mollie and I approached a familiar oak tree, bursting with these very hues, a gust of wind, seemingly out of nowhere, sent hundreds of leaves into the air, creating a dizzying visual display. After briefly twirling high above the trees, this vortex of color came to an abrupt halt as if it were suspended in time. Then, ever so gently, each leaf began to float down from the sky. Mesmerized by this scene, a poem I had written years ago came to mind:

God's confetti falling to the ground—red, yellow, orange,
I see all around. The colors of life on a canvas of gold—
the breath of nature is the story that is told.

Each time I look up at the trees or hear leaves crunch under my feet, it reminds me of the miraculous power of change. The constant ebb and flow of life can be thrilling, sometimes scary, and even worse, heartbreaking. When change occurs, something always has to die—a dream, a relationship, old habits, and even those we love. Like the leaves this time of year, each of life's transitions exposes its true colors before departing. Change is real. It is also forever.

As Mollie and I continued our way across town, I reflected on the changes that had taken place over the past year. Cara and I had experienced several, but they were minor compared to those around us. During the past 12 months, we'd watched family and friends deal with health issues, job loss, divorce, and a variety of other challenges. But there was one

❧

change, in October 2011, that ensured our lives would never be the same—a bittersweet conversion wrapped in a blanket of hope, love, faith, and loss.

When Cara and I met Alec and Heather, we immediately fell in love with them. Both were so warm, easygoing, and a constant reminder of what matters most. Blissfully married for just a few years, they were now eagerly waiting for their miracle to arrive, as Heather was in the seventh month of her pregnancy. Up until this point, their only "child" was Millie, a beautiful and well-trained golden retriever. Alec, who was an avid outdoorsman, had trained her to be his hunting and fishing companion. And she was. But Millie became so much more.

Here is a post from Heather's blog during the summer of 2012, honoring Millie on her birthday:

> *Today Millie turned five.*
>
> *I was thinking today, how much has happened in five years. We bought a house, got Millie, got engaged, got married, Alec was diagnosed with cancer, we had a baby, Alec died. And Millie was there, every step of the way. She would be the one to greet us, as we walked through the door after countless, long, grueling days of chemo, radiation, and doctors appointments. No matter what, she would brighten our spirits and force us to get outside and take her for a walk. There was nothing*

Millie wanted more in life than to be with her family outside, together. To her it was that simple.

Sometimes, I wish I could tell her how much she meant to Alec. Before we went to pick her out, he began researching how to train goldens. And he chose the "Cesar Millan" way, using the familiar "tsst!" sound toward Millie (and sometimes me!) every time she got out of line. Millie is probably the most well-trained dog in all of Maine. She never needs a leash; she comes when she is called; she is so good with our baby boy; and she doesn't jump, bark, or beg. She may steal your socks and bury them in the dirt, and nudge her head in inappropriate places (especially for men), but she is otherwise perfect.

Alec took so much pride in training Millie. Although she was my idea (Alec wanted a German shorthaired pointer for hunting), she was ultimately Alec's dog, giving new meaning to the phrase "man's best friend." He brought her everywhere, in his truck, out on the boat; no matter what, Millie was always by his side.

I have a million memories of Alec and Millie together hunting, skiing, fishing, hiking, biking—we always made sure she could come along. One of my favorite memories of Millie and Alec was when we were coming home from Alec's liver and lung surgery. He was in a lot of pain and barely able to move. When Millie first saw him (after 11 days of him being in the hospital), instead of wagging, jumping, or whimpering for joy of being reunited with her master, she came up to him ever so gently, licked his face, and carefully placed her head on his lap. She knew that he was hurting, and she was so gentle and peaceful. It was a beautiful moment between man and his best friend.

Millie would sleep next to me on the floor in her L.L.Bean bed. When I got up during the night, I would carefully have to walk around her. That later changed as Alec became sick. She started to lie near his side of the bed, and she stayed there for the remainder of his life . . . never leaving his side.

One day, my son and I were watching the slide-show videos I had made of Alec. I was pointing out "Da-da," and Millie ran over to the window, so excited, as if she was expecting to see Alec pull up in his truck and jump out. It broke my heart; I hope she knows he didn't want to leave her, either. He loved her, too.

Millie keeps me going; I have to get her exercised, and whether it's a walk or a run, we don't miss a day. Millie watches over my son and me. As a protective guard dog, she is always letting me know when someone pulls in our driveway, she sits by the stroller at all times, and she never runs too far ahead without checking on us during our walks. She always seems to be right there when I need her most, and I think she cries with me.

No one will ever replace Alec to her; he was her master, and I do believe dogs mourn, too. I know that we will all be together again someday. . . .

On the day of Alec's funeral, I stood at a quiet three-way intersection directing cars to our tiny seaside church. Most of the people attending were from out of state. They were also barely 30 years old. It was difficult to see so many young faces. As each car drove by, it was a sad reminder that regardless of one's age, impermanence is life's foremost guarantee. From the day we are born we sign an agreement, a spiritual contract, which is essentially a round-trip ticket back "home."

For Alec, his journey was brief, 35 years. But, over those three-and-a-half decades, he lived and loved more deeply than most. He also never wasted a single day complaining or asking "Why me?" He was much too busy loving his wife, new son, family, and friends. He proved that this is the one place that death loses and the soul wins: unlike the physical self, *love is forever.* Cancer may have taken Alec's body, but it could not take his spirit or the memories he holds of us . . . and we have of him.

Sometimes I wonder if we're all just here on vacation, taking in the endless sights that are offered to us along the way as we make the long walk home.

Granted, the sights are not always pretty, but as I've learned from Heather, eventually we must move forward. Holding on to the pain from our past is like driving through life staring into the rearview mirror. Sooner or later, we'll crash. Heather has shown everyone around her that one can go through a devastating loss and still live with grace, and eventually even joy. From where I stand, the greatest difference I see between this woman and those who remain paralyzed by their hardships is one word: *Yes*.

Although it hasn't been easy for her, Heather has chosen to celebrate and honor Alec's life by living her own. On any given day, if you ask, "Hey, Heather, want to go for a bike ride/go for a walk/go to the beach/grab an ice cream/do a triathlon/go fishing/hang out," the answer is invariably "Yes!" Rather than choosing no, which closes the heart and can be a thief to infinite possibilities, Heather's ability to remain open has allowed her to heal, while also inspiring others.

Since it was such a beautiful night, I decided to take Mollie on a longer route. Walking through the streets, we stopped to look at a dimly lit yard displaying carved pumpkins on the lawn and several bedsheet ghosts dangling from a tree. Scenes like this are another reason why October is my favorite month of the year. There's a mystical quality that surrounds it. Everything from haunted hayrides to apple picking and candy corn, these 31 days always bring out the kid in me. I remember when I was a little boy. The days leading up to Halloween had me feeling both excited . . . and terrified. I loved dressing up in costumes and filling my Star Wars pillowcase with treats as I went door-to-door, but I'd watched too many scary movies when my parents weren't looking. So before approaching each home while trick-or-treating, I always peeked behind the bushes, thoroughly convinced that a zombielike fiend would grab me, or, at the very least, one of the older kids in our neighborhood would steal my hard-earned candy.

Life often makes us feel as if we're fearfully waiting for some monster that's been conjured up in our imagination to grab us, stealing our collected treasures. But rarely does this happen. Perhaps if we're going to fear something, it should be that we're not fully living. I remember being asked by a friend, "If your doctor told you that you were going to die soon, what would you do? How would you live? Would you love more freely?"

Reflecting for a moment before responding, I finally said, "I'd probably live fearlessly, attempting anything and everything I've always wanted to do. I'd also stop worrying and being upset about the little things. And yes, I'd definitely love like there was no tomorrow—even the people I don't usually connect with."

He then said something so simple yet so frightening and profound that I will never forget it: "Well, I've got news for you, friend. It's happening this very second . . . you and I are dying, right now."

This is the paradox—we are living and dying in the same breath. Like the changing seasons, each of us is celebrating and mourning our existence. *We* are God's confetti. Once we accept this natural phenomenon, it allows us the freedom to love more deeply and encourages us to live for today.

As the sun was going down, I was reflecting on the past summer and the lessons I'd learned from Mollie. There had been many. But perhaps the greatest realization I've made since beginning our journey together is this: The essence of love isn't in the giving or receiving; it's in the *being*. Being love is what allows Mollie to see beauty and goodness in all that exists. She never "tries" to love; she only expresses her true, divine nature; the same nature that flows through you and me. From this vantage point, the notion of loving everyone no longer seems radical. It just seems natural.

After walking for nearly an hour, Mollie and I were now just minutes from our house, and turning the corner onto our street triggered something inside of me. I started to contemplate the numerous sidewalks, roads, and neighborhoods we'd traversed throughout the last several months. Some were quiet and picturesque, while others had been noisy, even a little rough at times. Although each one took us in a different direction, they always led us back to the same place: home.

Now standing at the foot of our stairs, I looked at Mollie and said, "Good job, girl. I'm proud of you; that was a long walk!" While giving her praise, she stared up at me as if she understood every word. Bending down, I wrapped my arms around her neck and said, "I love you, Mollie."

She then pressed her body close to mine and rested her head on my shoulder as if to say, "I love you, too, Daddy."

Acknowledgments

First and foremost, I want to thank my amazing, beautiful (and extremely patient) wife, Cara, for always believing in me. I am truly grateful for your constant love and support. Your heart and creative input can be found on every page of this book, and it's another reminder of why I love you so much.

My deepest gratitude to my family and friends who have been so encouraging and supportive while I wrote this book: my mom, Patty; stepdad, Scott; my son, Alex; my editor and dear friend, October Craig; Lisa and Michael Hallahan; Kevin Cote; Mike McDonald; Susan Mullen; Bill and Karen Auld; Shawn Jarvis; Kris Wittenberg; Marie Ciccarone; John and Marti Odle; Reverend Jan Hyrniewicz; and the wonderful people at Union Church. Special thanks to John, Mike, Heather, and Ann: your wisdom and powerful stories have changed my life.

A huge shout-out to Dr. Brion Reagor and the extraordinary staff at Lucky Pet Animal Hospital: Mollie is truly *lucky* to have you! *Woof!*

To my family at Hay House: thank you Reid Tracy for another opportunity to work with the world's best publisher. To Patrick Gabrysiak, Shannon Littrell, and Christy Salinas . . . thank you for your ideas and talents. Also sending much love and gratitude to my friend and mentor, Louise Hay. Your kindness toward me means more than you could ever know.

And to Mollie . . . my sweet, loving, beautiful, and crazy girl: Your spirit is unlike any two- or four-legged creature this world has ever seen. Thank you for showing me the true meaning of love and devotion and for choosing to be a part of our family. I love you.

Most of all, I thank God for my amazing life and the freedom to live each day off the leash. I am truly one lucky dog.

ABOUT THE AUTHOR

Michael J. Chase is an author, inspirational speaker and student of spiritual wisdom, both ancient and contemporary. Considered an expert on the subjects of kindness and positive behaviour, he is one of today's most sought-after teachers in the field of personal and spiritual development. As founder of The Kindness Center, Michael, along with his teachings, is recognized across the globe. Whether he's sharing his insights in a classroom, in a boardroom or onstage in front of thousands of people, his powerful message impacts countless lives each year. Michael lives in Maine with his wife, son, and best friend Mollie.

www.michaeljchase.com

We hope you enjoyed this Hay House book. If you'd like to receive our online catalogue featuring additional information on Hay House books and products, or if you'd like to find out more about the Hay Foundation, please contact:

Hay House UK, Ltd., Astley House, 33 Notting Hill Gate, London W11 3JQ
Phone: 0-20-3675-2450 • *Fax:* 0-20-3675-2451
www.hayhouse.co.uk • **www.hayfoundation.org**

Published and distributed in the United States by:
Hay House, Inc., P.O. Box 5100, Carlsbad, CA 92018-5100
Phone: (760) 431-7695 or (800) 654-5126
Fax: (760) 431-6948 or (800) 650-5115
www.hayhouse.com®

Published and distributed in Australia by: Hay House Australia Pty. Ltd.,
18/36 Ralph St., Alexandria NSW 2015 • *Phone:* 612-9669-4299
Fax: 612-9669-4144 • www.hayhouse.com.au

Published and distributed in the Republic of South Africa by: Hay House
SA (Pty), Ltd., P.O. Box 990, Witkoppen 2068 • *Phone/Fax:* 27-11-467-8904
www.hayhouse.co.za

Published in India by: Hay House Publishers India, Muskaan Complex,
Plot No. 3, B-2, Vasant Kunj, New Delhi 110 070 • *Phone:* 91-11-4176-1620
Fax: 91-11-4176-1630 • www.hayhouse.co.in

Distributed in Canada by: Raincoast, 9050 Shaughnessy St., Vancouver,
B.C. V6P 6E5 • *Phone:* (604) 323-7100 • *Fax:* (604) 323-2600
www.raincoast.com

Take Your Soul on a Vacation

Visit **www.HealYourLife.com®** to regroup, recharge, and reconnect with
your own magnificence. Featuring blogs, mind-body-spirit news, and life-
changing wisdom from Louise Hay and friends.

Visit **www.HealYourLife.com** today!